Development of the Industrial U.S.

Reference Library Cumulative Index

Development of the Industrial U.S.

Reference Library Cumulative Index

Jennifer York Stock,
Index Coordinator

U·X·L
A part of Gale, Cengage Learning

GALE
CENGAGE Learning

Detroit • New York • San Francisco • New Haven, Conn • Waterville, Maine • London

GALE
CENGAGE Learning

Development of the Industrial U.S: Cumulative Index

Index Coordinator
Jennifer York Stock

Rights Acquisitions and Management
Shalice Shah-Caldwell, Kim Smilay

Imaging and Multimedia
Randy Bassett, Lezlie Light, Daniel Newell, Denay Wilding

Product Design
Pamela A. E. Galbreath

Composition
Evi Seoud

Manufacturing
Rita Wimberley

For more information, contact:
Gale
27500 Drake Rd.
Farmington Hills, MI 48331-3535
Or you can visit our Internet site at
gale.cengage.com

Cover photographs of Eli Whitney's cotton gin, © Bettmann/Corbis; a young girl standing at a spinning machine in a textile factory, © Bettmann/Corbis; Jane Addams, courtesy of The Library of Congress.

LIBRARY OF CONGRESS CATALOGING-IN-PUBLICATION DATA

Library of Congress Cataloging-in-Publication Data
Development of the industrial U.S. reference library cumulative index / Jennifer York Stock, index coordinator.
p. cm.
Cumulates indexes for Development of the industrial U.S., issued in three parts; Almanac, Biographies, and Primary sources, by Sonia G. Benson.
ISBN 1-4144-0180-9 (softcover)
1. Industries--United States--History--Juvenile literature--Indexes. 2. Industrial revolution--United States--History--Juvenile literature--Indexes.
[1. United States-- Economic conditions--To 1865--Juvenile literature--Indexes.]
I. Stock, Jennifer York, 1974- II. Benson, Sonia. Development of the industrial U.S.

HC105.D47 2006
338.0973--dc22 2005016351

Printed in the United States of America
4 5 6 7 8 9 15 14 13 12 11 10 09

Cumulative Index

A = Development of the Industrial U.S.: Almanac
B = Development of the Industrial U.S.: Biographies
PS = Development of the Industrial U.S.: Primary Sources

Bold italic type indicates abbreviation of individual titles.

Bold type indicates major ***Biographies*** or ***Primary Sources*** entries.

Illustrations are marked by (ill.).

A

Aaseng, Nathan
  B: 131
Abbott, Lyman
  A: 77
Accessory Transit Company (ATC)
  B: 239
Accommodationism
  B: 250
Adams, Ansel
  PS: 107
Adams, Charles Francis
  A: 66
  PS: 61
  as minister to Great Britain, ***PS:*** 62
Adams, Charles Francis, Jr.
  PS: 69
  as author with brother of *A Chapter of Erie,* ***PS:*** 69
Adams, Henry Brooks
  PS: 61–70, 63 (ill.)
  as author with brother of *A Chapter of Erie,* ***PS:*** 69
  awarding of Pulitzer Prize for *The Education of Henry Adams: An Autobiography,* ***PS:*** 69
  books written by, ***PS:*** 63–64
  early life of, ***PS:*** 61–62
  as editor of *North American Review,* ***PS:*** 63
  education of, ***PS:*** 61
  excerpt from *The Education of Henry Adams: An Autobiography* by, ***PS:*** 67–69
  as reporter for the *Nation,* ***PS:*** 62–63
Adams, John
  PS: 61
Adams, John Quincy
  PS: 61
Addams, Ann Haldeman
  B: 3
Addams, Jane
  A: 123
  B: **1–9,** 2 (ill.), 6 (ill.), 104
  achievements of, ***B:*** 1, 9
  as delegate to Progressive political party national convention, ***B:*** 7
  early life and education of, ***B:*** 2–3
  Ellen Gates Starr and, ***B:*** 216–18, 220

founding of Hull House by, **B:** 1, 3–5, 100, 120, 121–22, 215, 218, 220
opposition to World War I, **B:** 9
settlement movement and, **A:** 112
Addams, John Huy
B: 2–3
Aerial Experiment Association
B: 28
Aertson, Jan
B: 234
African Americans
discrimination against, **A:** 108, 156
education of, **A:** 161–64
inventions by, **B:** 178–79
labor movement and, **B:** 189
in labor unions, **A:** 149–50
migration of, **A:** 107–8, 163
African Methodist Episcopal (AME) Church
B: 183, 247
Age of Reason
PS: 89
Agriculture. *See also* Farming
Farmers' Alliance and, **A:** 178–79
Grange and, **A:** 175–77, 176 (ill.)
inventions and, **A:** 169–71
Jefferson's pro view of, **A:** 9
sharecropping in, **A:** 159–60
Southern Alliance and, **A:** 164–65
tenant farming in, **A:** 159–60
Air brakes
A: 78
Albany and Susquehanna Railroad
B: 166
Alexander, Alland, Sr.
PS: 107
Alger, Horatio
PS: 181–92, 185 (ill.)
excerpt from *Ragged Dick, or, Street Life in New York with the Boot-Blacks* by, **PS:** 187–90
interest in helping poor urban children, **PS:** 183–84
moralistic tone of writing, **PS:** 185, 191
novels of, **PS:** 184–85
rags-to-riches themes of, **A:** 57; **PS:** 181, 192, 205
Alger, Horatio, Association of Distinguished Americans
PS: 191
Alien poll tax
PS: 73
All in a Day's Work (Tarbell)
B: 229
PS: 129
Allegheny Mountains
PS: 49
Allgemeine Elektriziåts Gesellschaft (AEG)
B: 95
Almy and Brown textile firm
A: 11
Almy, William
B: 211
Alternating current (AC)
B: 69
Altgeld, John P.
B: 105–6, 122
Amalgamated Association of Iron and Steel Workers (AAISW)
A: 92–93, 146–47, 148
B: 35
American Anti Slavery Society
B: 179
American Association for the Advancement of Science
B: 28
American Association for the Promotion of the Teaching of Speech to the Deaf
B: 27
American Civil War (1861–65)
PS: 13
African American inventors before, **B:** 178–79
destruction in, **A:** 155
impact of, on industrialization, **A:** 2, 63
Lease on, **B:** 137
Republican legislation during, **A:** 59–62
slavery as issue in, **A:** 1–2, 39, 107–8; **B:** 156, 196
Union navy in, **B:** 130
American Federation of Labor (AFL)
A: 144, 145, 146
B: 55, 189
PS: 175, 179 (ill.)
support for La Follette, **B:** 119
American Federation of Labor and Congress of Industrial Organizations (AFL-CIO)
B: 190
American Fur Company
B: 12
American Industrial Revolution
B: 211
American League of Colored Laborers
B: 189
American Missionary Association
B: 246
American Museum of Natural History
A: 94
American Notes and Pictures from Italy (Dickens)
PS: 42
American Railway Union (ARU)
A: 144, 146
establishment of, **B:** 52
support for Pullman strike, **B:** 53
American Red Cross
B: 205
American Revolution (1775–83)
A: 1, 14
B: 73, 148, 215
American Society of Mechanical Engineers (ASME)
B: 93, 98
American system
A: 30–35
American Telephone & Telegraph Company (AT&T)
B: 26, 28
PS: 90
American Tobacco Company
A: 158–59, 189
breakup of, **PS:** 94
Amoskeag Falls facility
B: 212
An Enquiry into the Principles on Which a Commercial System for the United States of America Should be Founded (Coxe)
PS: 12–13

A = Development of the Industrial U.S.: Almanac—
B = Development of the Industrial U.S.: Biographies

An Inquiry into the Nature and Causes of the Wealth of Nations (Smith)
A: 62–63
PS: 117
Anarchists
A: 142
Anderson, Sarah
B: 217
Anthony, Susan B.
PS: 48
Anti-Asian sentiments, against Chinese immigrants
A: 73, 105–6
Anti-Asian violence
PS: 76–77
Anti-Chinese riot (1880)
PS: 81 (ill.)
Anti-immigrant discrimination
PS: 71
Antitrust movement
Clayton Antitrust Act in, *A:* 192–93; *PS:* 158
under Cleveland, Grover, *A:* 99
under Harrison, Benjamin, *A:* 99
in Kansas, *A:* 98
under McKinley, William, *A:* 99
under Roosevelt, Theodore, *A:* 187–89; *B:* 115–16, 171; *PS:* 157, 158
Sherman Antitrust Act in, *A:* 98–99, 148, 184, 188–89; *B:* 170, 171, 202, 203, 227–28; *PS:* 94, 116, 121, 144, 145, 149, 153–59
state legislation on, *PS:* 152
under Taft, William Howard, *PS:* 158
Antitrust Political Cartoons
***PS:* 136–46**
"A Trust Giant's Point of View" (ill.), *PS:* 144
"A Trustworthy Beast" (ill.), *PS:* 143
Apple Computers
PS: 159
Apprentices
A: 11, 28
in machine shop, *A:* 29 (ill.)
Arapaho Indians
A: 170
Arc lights
B: 67
Architecture, Commercial Style of
A: 115
Arkwright Mills
B: 149
Arkwright, Richard
A: 4, 11
B: 149, 209–10, 210 (ill.)
Armed Neutrality Bill
B: 116
Armour Institute of Technology
A: 94
Armour Mission
A: 94
Armour, Philip Danforth
A: 94
Armstrong, Samuel Chapman
A: 161
B: 247
Art Resources in Teaching (ART)
B: 221
Articles of Confederation
PS: 11–12
Assembly line
A: 203
Association of Black Caulkers
B: 189
Astor, Caroline Webster Schermerhorn
A: 108
***B:* 10–19**, 11 (ill.)
death of, *B:* 19
decline of social life, *B:* 18–19
early life of, *B:* 11–12
family life of, *B:* 13
insistence on being called "Mrs. Astor," *B:* 11, 18
list of 400 and, *B:* 13–15, 16, 17
marriage to William Backhouse Astor Jr., *B:* 12, 13
in Newport, Rhode Island, *B:* 13, 19
social balls of, *B:* 14, 15–18
Astor, Carrie
B: 17–18
Astor, John Jacob
B: 12
Astor, John Jacob, III
B: 13
Astor, John Jacob, IV
B: 13, 18
Astor, Mary
B: 18
Astor, William Backhouse, Jr.
B: 12, 13, 18
Astor, William Backhouse, Sr.
B: 12–13
Astor, William Waldorf
B: 18
Atgeld, John P.
B: 123 (ill.)
Atlanta Compromise
A: 162
B: 250–51
Atlantic Monthly (magazine)
A: 185
PS: 94, 116
founding of, *PS:* 195
Howells as editor of, *PS:* 195–96
Automatic engine lubricator
B: 156–58, 157 (ill.)
Avondale mining disaster
A: 131

B

Baby Bells
B: 28
Bachelor society
A: 106
Bagley, Sarah
PS: 41, 42, 47
Baker, Josephine L.
PS: 42
excerpt from "A Second Peep at Factory Life" by, *PS:* 43–46
Baker, Ray Stannard
B: 54–55
Bakeshop Act (New York, 1895)
A: 193–94
Baltimore & Ohio (B & O) Railroad
A: 79
PS: 58
1877 strike of, *A:* 80 (ill.)
locomotive for, *A:* 21–22, 21 (ill.)
Baltimore, Maryland
A: 102
Bank failures
B: 167
Bank of the United States
PS: 12
Banknotes
B: 172

Banneker, Benjamin
B: 178
Barbed wire
A: 173, 174 (ill.)
Barge Canal System
PS: 59
Barnard Cloisters
B: 200
Barnett, Samuel A.
B: 3–4
Barnor, Albert
B: 150
Bartering
A: 168, 169
Barthel, Oliver E.
B: 82
Bartram, John
B: 101, 102
Bartram, Margaret
B: 102
Bartram, Nicholas
B: 102
Bathrooms
A: 114
Beechwood
B: 19
Beinn Bhreagh
B: 28
Belknap, William W.
PS: 63
Bell, Alexander Graham
B: 21–28, 22 (ill.)
PS: 90
advocation of enforced sterilization, **B:** 27–28
family background of, **B:** 21–23
focus on teaching of deaf, **B:** 21, 23–24, 27, 131
invention of telephone, **B:** 21, 27–28
inventions and achievements of, **B:** 28
life in Boston, **B:** 23–24
patents of, **B:** 24–26
as recipient of Volta Prize, **B:** 27
work with Edison, **B:** 60, 65
work with Latimer, **B:** 128, 130–32
work with Watson, **B:** 24–26
writings of, **B:** 27
Bell, Alexander (grandfather), death of
B: 23
Bell, Alexander Melville
B: 21–22
Bell, Edward
B: 23
Bell, Melly
B: 23
Bell, Melville
B: 23
Bell Telephone Company
B: 26, 28
PS: 90
Bennett, Harry H.
B: 88
Benz, Karl
B: 81
Bessemer converter
A: 78
Bessemer, Henry
A: 78, 91
B: 33
PS: 138
steel production system of, **PS:** 138–39
Bessemer method
B: 33
Bessemer Steamship Company
B: 169
Bessemer's system
PS: 139
Big business
drive to regulate, **A:** 184–85
growth of, **A:** 60–61
Black Codes
B: 250
Black Friday
A: 66
PS: 66
Black lung
A: 129
Blair, Henry T.
B: 179
Blanchard, Isaac G.,
PS: 174, 180
lyrics of "Eight Hours" (song) by, **PS:** 176–78,
Blanck (Triangle Shirtwaist Factory owner)
PS: 168
Bloomer, Amelia
PS: 47, 47 (ill.)
Board of Patent Control
B: 134
Boeing, William
A: 210
Bonds
A: 61
sale of Northern Pacific to public, **A:** 77
Bonsack Company
A: 158
Bonsall, Caroline Bartram
B: 100–1
Boot industry
A: 52–55, 54 (ill.)
Booth, Charles
B: 105
Boston Associates
A: 46–47, 48, 50
B: 148–49
Boston Brahmans
PS: 195
Boston Eight Hour League
PS: 176
Boston Manufacturing Company
A: 46–47
B: 151–52, 152 (ill.)
organization of, **B:** 148–49
Boston, Massachusetts
A: 102
immigrant populations in, **PS:** 101
streetcars in, **A:** 107
Boulton & Watt steam engine
B: 75
Boulton, Matthew
B: 74
Boycotts
B: 53
Brace, Charles Loring
PS: 191, 192
Brandeis, Louis D.
PS: 178, 179 (ill.)
Breaker boys
A: 129–30, 130 (ill.)
Breckinridge, Sophonisba
B: 125
Brinkley, Douglas
B: 80, 85, 88
Bronchitis
A: 121–22
Brotherhood of Locomotive Firemen (BLF)
B: 51
Brotherhood of Railway and Airline Clerks
B: 192

Brotherhood of Sleeping Car Porters (BSCP)
A: 150
B: 182, 186–87
Brothers Machine Shop
B: 81
Brown, John
B: 160
Brown, Moses
A: 11
B: 148–49, 211–12
Brown, Moses, School
B: 149
Brown, Obadiah
B: 148
Brown University
B: 149, 211
Brown, W. C.
B: 130
Brownlow, Henry
B: 160
Bryan, William Jennings
A: 180
B: 141 (ill.)
in election of 1896, ***B:*** 140–41, 142
Bryn Mawr Summer School for Women Workers
PS: 169
Buddhism
B: 42
Buffalo, extermination of
A: 170–71
Buffalo, New York
PS: 53
Bull Moose Party
A: 192
Bunyan, John
B: 229
Burlingame Treaty (1868)
PS: 74
Burr, Aaron
PS: 19
Burroughs, James
B: 244
Business of Being a Woman, The (Tarbell)
B: 232
Business pools
PS: 118
Business. *See* Big business; Corporations
Butler, Edward
B: 218
Butler, Nicholas Murray
B: 9
Butte, Montana
A: 178

C

Cable News Network (CNN)
B: 242
Cabot, Susanna
B: 144
California Constitution, as anti Chinese
PS: 80–81
California gold rush
B: 43, 238–39
Camden and Amboy Railroad
A: 24
Canadian Southern Railroad
B: 241
The Canal Boat
***PS:* 49–60**
excerpt from "The Canal Boat" (Hawthorne), ***PS:*** 54–57
Canals
A: 19–20
Capital
A: 8, 22, 63–64, 88
Capitalism
A: 64, 108, 143
Carding
A: 12
machines for, ***A:*** 47
Carey, Ernestine Gilbreth
B: 96
Carnegie, Andrew
A: 64, 129, 146, 163
***B:* 30–39**, 31 (ill.)
PS: 94, 138–39, 148, 181
background, ***B:*** 31–32
Carnegie Steel and, ***PS:*** 138–39
Civil War and, ***B:*** 32
creation of pension fund for workers, ***B:*** 36–37
donations to Tuskegee Institute by, ***B:*** 252
early life of, ***PS:*** 138
family life of, ***B:*** 38–39
gospel of wealth and, ***A:*** 94–95
Homestead Strike and, ***A:*** 92–93; ***B:*** 35–36
interest in steel industry, ***B:*** 33–35
investments of, ***B:*** 33
J. P. Morgan and, ***B:*** 169
legacy of, ***B:*** 30
partnership with Frick, ***B:*** 34, 35
at Pennsylvania Railroad, ***A:*** 91–92
philanthropy of, ***A:*** 94; ***B:*** 30, 35–36, 38–39; ***PS:*** 146
purchase of Homestead Works, ***B:*** 34–35
sale of Carnegie Steel, ***A:*** 95
sale of Homestead Works to Morgan, ***B:*** 36
spelling reform and, ***B:*** 37
as target of political cartoons, ***PS:*** 137–38, 142, 143, 143 (ill.)
wealth of, ***PS:*** 88
work with Pennsylvania Railroad, ***B:*** 32–33
Carnegie Corporation
A: 94
B: 39
PS: 146
Carnegie Endowment for International Peace
A: 94
PS: 146
Carnegie Foundation for the Advancement of Teaching
A: 94
B: 39
PS: 146
Carnegie Hall
A: 94
B: 38
PS: 146
Carnegie Institute of Technology
A: 94
B: 39
PS: 146
Carnegie, Louise
B: 38, 39
Carnegie, Margaret
B: 32, 38, 39
Carnegie, McCandless, and Company
B: 33

Carnegie Steel
A: 92, 95, 146–47
B: 34, 37, 169
PS: 138–39
Morgan's purchase of, *PS:* 144–45
as target of political cartoons, *PS:* 137–38
Carnegie Teachers' Pension Fund
B: 38
Carnegie, Thomas
B: 32
Carnegie, William
B: 31–32
Carnegie-Mellon University
A: 94
B: 39
PS: 146
Carver, George Washington
B: 248
Casement, Jack
A: 72
Cashman, Dennis
A: 156
Cattle drives
A: 173
Cattle industry
A: 172–75
Caucus system
B: 113, 114
Census Bureau
A: 212
Central business district
A: 104
Central Pacific Railroad
B: 44–45, 46–47
PS: 73
Central Pacific Railroad Company
A: 71, 74, 106
construction of, *A:* 73–74
Century Illustrated Monthly Magazine
PS: 197
Chapter of Erie, A (Adams and Adams)
PS: 69
Charleston, South Carolina, damage to, in American Civil War
A: 155
Chautauquan (magazine)
B: 226
PS: 127
Cheaper by the Dozen (Gilbreth)
B: 96
Chernow, Ron
B: 197
PS: 113, 117, 122–23, 124
Chesapeake and Ohio Canal
PS: 58
Chevron
B: 203
Cheyenne Indians
A: 170
Chicago and Alton Railroad
A: 81
Chicago, Burlington, & Quincy Railroad
A: 187, 188
B: 170
Chicago, Illinois
Addams's move to, *B:* 4–5
Board of Trade in, *A:* 168
garment industry in, *A:* 127
great fire in, *A:* 115; *B:* 217–18
growth of, *A:* 20, 167; *PS:* 53
Haymarket Square Riot in, *A:* 141–43, 142 (ill.)
Hull House in, *A:* 112; *B:* 1, 3–5, 100, 120, 121–22, 215, 218, 219
immigrant populations in, *PS:* 101
immigrants in, *A:* 105
living conditions in, *B:* 5–7, 54, 122
meatpacking in, *A:* 88, 163; *B:* 4
population of, *A:* 102
rebuilding of, after fire, *A:* 115
typhoid epidemic in, *B:* 8
Chicago Institute of Social Science
B: 125
Chicago Record (newspaper)
B: 54
Chicago School of Architects
A: 115
Chicago, University of
A: 94
B: 204–5
PS: 122
Child, the Clinic and the Court, The (Lathrop)
B: 126
Child labor
A: 11, 45, 121–25, 122 (ill.), 194–95, 194 (ill.)
B: 116, 213–14
Kelley's work on, *B:* 100, 104
Lathrop's efforts to end, *B:* 126
reform of, *A:* 122–25
in textile industry, *PS:* 15
Children's Aid Society
PS: 183, 191
Children's Bureau
A: 124–25, 195
B: 106
establishment of, *A:* 124–25; *B:* 100
under Lathrop, *B:* 120, 125–26
China, life in
B: 40–41
Chinatowns
A: 106
B: 47
PS: 73, 74
gang attacks on, *PS:* 76–77
Chinese Consolidated Benevolent Association
PS: 75, 76
Chinese Exclusion Act (1882)
B: 47
PS: 81
repeal of, in 1943, *PS:* 81–82
Chinese immigrants
assimilation of, *A:* 106
in construction of Central Pacific, *A:* 73–74
discrimination against, *A:* 73, 105–6; *PS:* 71, 72–73, 72 (ill.), 75–76
life of, in San Francisco, *PS:* 75
mob attacks on, *PS:* 80
reliance on community support, *PS:* 74–75
settlement of, in Chinatowns, *PS:* 73, 74
work on the railroads, *PS:* 71, 73–74
Chinese Immigration Act (1882)
A: 106
Chinese Six Companies,
PS: 75, 76
text of "Memorial of the Chinese Six Companies to U.S. Grant, President of the United States" by, *PS:* 78–80
Chinese Transcontinental Railroad Workers
***B:* 40–48**
anti-Asian prejudice against, *B:* 44, 47

arrival in California, ***B:*** 43–45
immigration laws restricting, ***B:*** 47
reasons for immigrating, ***B:*** 41–43
religion of, ***B:*** 42–43
return to China, ***B:*** 48
trip to United States, ***B:*** 42
work in gold mines, ***B:*** 43–44
work on railroad, ***B:*** 44–47
Chisholm Trail
A: 173
Chrysler Corporation
B: 83
Church of the Strangers
B: 241
Cincinnati, Ohio, settlement of
A: 19
Cities. *See also* Urbanization
crime in, ***A:*** 110
department stores in, ***A:*** 115
early, ***A:*** 103–5
health and safety in, ***A:*** 109–10
immigrants in, ***A:*** 105, 126–27
improvements in, ***A:*** 112–14
political machines in, ***A:*** 110
reform of, ***A:*** 111–12
tenements in, ***A:*** 108–9, 109 (ill.)
Civil Aeronautics Act
A: 210
Civil Aeronautics Authority (CAA)
A: 210
Civil Rights Act (1964)
B: 189, 191
Clayton Antitrust Act (1914)
A: 192–93
PS: 158
Clermont (steamboat)
A: 18, 19 (ill.)
Cleveland, Grover
B: 54
PS: 148
antitrust policy under, ***A:*** 99
labor relations and, ***A:*** 145–46; ***B:*** 56–57
Cleveland Massacre
A: 90–91
PS: 113
Cleveland, Ohio
A: 20
immigrants in, ***A:*** 105
oil refineries in, ***A:*** 90–91
Cleveland, Ohio, growth of
PS: 53
Clinton, DeWitt
PS: 50
celebration on opening of Erie Canal, ***PS:*** 51–52
Clocks, Eli Terry's mass-produced
A: 34
Cloth merchants
A: 4
Clothing industry, ready-made
A: 50–51
Clyburn, James
B: 180
Coal mining
A: 129–31, 130 (ill.)
Coke
A: 4–5, 92
Cold War (1945–91)
B: 245
College of William and Mary
PS: 3
Collier's (magazine)
A: 185
B: 228
Colorado Fuel and Iron Company
B: 200
Colored Farmers' Alliance
A: 165
B: 177
Colored National Labor Union
A: 149
B: 189
Colt revolver
A: 35 (ill.) 39
Colt, Samuel
A: 35 (ill.)
firearms manufacturing of, ***A:*** 34
Commerce clause
PS: 153
Commerce, U.S. Department of, establishment of
A: 191
Commercial Style of architecture
A: 115
Communication
advances in, ***A:*** 23–24
telegraph in, ***A:*** 24–26, 26 (ill.)
Communist Manifesto, The (Marx and Engels)
A: 143
B: 102, 103
Competition
PS: 149, 150–51
in railroad business, ***A:*** 80, 82
trouble with free, ***A:*** 85–88
Computer age
A: 212–15
mass production in, ***A:*** 214–15
The Concentration of Wealth
PS: **84–96**
excerpt from *The Concentration of Wealth: Its Economic Justification* (Sumner), ***PS:*** 90–93
Conditions of the Working-class in England, The (Engels)
B: 102, 103
Conference on Social Work
B: 106
Confucianism
B: 42
Congress for Industrial Organization (CIO)
B: 189
Congressional Report on Manufacturers
A: 10
PS: **10–20**
accuracy of, ***PS:*** 13
Coxe as author of first draft, ***PS:*** 13, 18
excerpt from *Report to Congress on the Subject of Manufacturers* (Hamilton) ***PS:*** 15–18
Connelly, William E.
B: 139
Conscription
B: 190
Conservation movement, Theodore Roosevelt and
A: 190
Consolidation
A: 87
PS: 118
Conspicuous consumption
B: 16–17
Constitution, U.S.
commerce clause of, ***PS:*** 153
provision for patents in, ***A:*** 33; ***PS:*** 24–25
Constitutional Convention (1787)
B: 71, 237
Hamilton as delegate to, ***PS:*** 12
Jefferson as delegate to, ***PS:*** 1

Consumer action, Kelley's interest in
B: 106
Consumer industries
A: 206–7
Continental Army
B: 73, 76
Continental Congress
B: 75
Jefferson as delegate to, *PS:* 3
Contract Labor Law (1864)
A: 61–62
Conwell, Russell H.
A: 96
Cook County Juvenile Court
B: 124
establishment of, *B:* 126
Cooke, Jay
A: 61
panic of 1873 and, *A:* 76–77
Cooke, William Fothergill
A: 24–25
Coolidge, Calvin
B: 117
as pro-business president, *A:* 205
Cooper, Anderson
B: 242
Cooper, Carter
B: 242
Cooper, Wyatt
B: 242
Copeland, Vince
B: 229
Corbin, Abel R.
A: 66
Corning, New York, growth of
A: 103
Corporations
A: 22, 197
railroad, *A:* 21
Cosmopolitan (magazine)
B: 228
Cotton
cleaning of, *PS:* 22
United States export of, *PS:* 23
Cotton gin
A: 31, 36, 37 (ill.)
PS: 14, 22 (ill.)
invention of, *PS:* 21, 23
patent for, *PS:* 23–24
text of petition for patent for (Whitney), *PS:* 25–26
Cotton Gin Petition (Whitney)
***PS:* 21–29**
text of *PS:* 25–26
Cotton production
A: 36
Cotton States and International Exposition
A: 161–62
B: 180, 251
Cottonseed oil
A: 157
Coxe, Tench
PS: 12, 13 (ill.), 18
Crane, Stephen
PS: 196
Credit Mobilier scandal
PS: 63
Criticism and Fiction (Howells)
PS: 197
Crocker, Charles
A: 71, 73
B: 44, 46
Crosby and Gould (law firm)
B: 131
"Cross of Gold" speech (Bryan)
B: 141
Crystal Palace Exhibition (London, 1851)
A: 39–40, 40 (ill.)
Cumberland Road
A: 17
Curtis, Harriet F.
PS: 41

D

Daimler, Gottlieb
B: 81
Darwin, Charles
A: 95–96
PS: 86
evolution theory of, *PS:* 89
Davis, John W.
B: 117
Davis, Paulina Wright
PS: 47
Dayton, Ohio, growth of
A: 103
Deaf, teaching of
B: 21, 23–24, 27
Dearborn Independent (newspaper)
B: 86
Dearborn, Michigan
B: 80
Debs, Daniel
B: 50–51
Debs, Eugene Victor
A: 144–45, 146, 148
***B:* 49–59**, 57 (ill.), 58 (ill.)
campaigns for president, *B:* 57–59
childhood of, *B:* 50–51
creation of Social Democratic Party, *B:* 57
as Democrat, *B:* 51, 56
early union work, *B:* 51–52
in election of 1912, *A:* 192
in establishing American Railway Union, *B:* 52
illness and death of, *B:* 59
as Indiana member of House of Representatives, *B:* 51
opposition to World War I, *B:* 58
prison sentences of, *B:* 56, 58–59
Pullman strike and, *B:* 52–56
socialism and, *B:* 56–57
Debs, Kate Metzel
B: 51
Debs, Marguerite
B: 50–51
Declaration of Independence (1776)
PS: 3
Deere, John
A: 169, 170
steel plow of, *A:* 38–39
Defender (newspaper)
A: 163
Delaney, Eliza Montgomery
B: 160
Delaney, Jacob
B: 160
Delaware Indians
B: 73–74
Democratic Party
B: 51, 56
backing of agricultural and slave-based economy by, *A:* 59
Lease on, *B:* 137
Democratic republic
A: 8
Democratic-Republicans
PS: 7–8, 19

Denver, Colorado
A: 178
Depression of 1893–96
B: 19, 35
Depression(s)
of 1873, *A:* 137–39
economic, *A:* 8, 106–7
Great, *A:* 206–7
Detroit Automobile Company
A: 201–2
B: 82, 83
Detroit Drydock Company
B: 81
Detroit, Michigan
growth and development of, *A:* 20; *B:* 83; *PS:* 53
immigrants in, *A:* 105
Dewey Decimal System
B: 37
Dewey, John, visits by, to Hull House
B: 7–8
Dewey, Melvil
B: 37
Dickens, Charles
A: 49
PS: 42–43, 43 (ill.)
Direct current (DC)
B: 69
Direct primaries
B: 113, 114
Discrimination
against African Americans, *A:* 108, 156
against Chinese Americans, *A:* 73, 105–6; *PS:* 71, 72–73 72 (ill.), 75–76
Douglas, Donald
A: 210
Douglass, Frederick
B: 134
Downsizing
A: 215
Drew, Daniel
A: 74
B: 238, 239–40
PS: 66
Drexel, Morgan and Company
B: 165
Dry plate process
PS: 106
DuBois, W. E. B.
A: 164
B: 250, 251
Dudley, Massachusetts, factory compound in
A: 45
Duke, James Buchanan
A: 158 (ill.)
breakup of American Tobacco Company of, *PS:* 94
tobacco industry and, *A:* 157–59
Duke Power Company
A: 159
Duke University
A: 159
Duke, W., Sons and Company
A: 158
Duke, Washington
A: 157
Duncan, Sherman & Company
B: 164
Durant, Thomas C.
A: 71, 74
Duryea, Charles E.
B: 81
Duryea, J. Frank
B: 81
Dutch West Indies Company
B: 12
Dynamo
PS: 62 (ill.)
Dyslexia
B: 62

E

Eastman Dry Plate Company
PS: 106
Eastman, George
A: 163
B: 252
PS: 106
Eastman Kodak
B: 95
PS: 106
Economic depressions
A: 8, 106–7
Economy
capital in, *A:* 63–64
laissez-faire policy in, *A:* 62–63, 85, 122, 131, 182
pre–Civil War, *A:* 153–55, 153 (ill.)
Edison effect
B: 69
Edison Electric Light Company
B: 67
Edison General Electric Light Company
B: 68–70, 133
formation of, *B:* 68–70
Edison Illuminating Company
B: 82
Edison, Mary Stilwell
B: 65, 69
Edison, Mina Miller
B: 69
Edison, Nancy
B: 61, 62
Edison, Samuel
B: 60–61
Edison, Thomas
A: 113, 114 (ill.)
***B:* 60–70**, 61 (ill.)
Bell's improvement to phonograph invention by, *B:* 27
contributions to motion picture industry, *B:* 68–69
death of, *B:* 70
early jobs of, *B:* 62
early life of, *B:* 60–61
Edison effect and, *B:* 69
education of, *B:* 61–62
establishment of Greenfield Village, *B:* 69–70
Ford and, *B:* 83
formation of Edison General Electric Company, *B:* 68–70
inventions of, *B:* 65–68, 131
J. P. Morgan and, *B:* 169
laboratory of, *B:* 65
Latimer and, *B:* 128, 133
legacy of, *B:* 70
move to Menlo Park, New Jersey, *B:* 65–68
patents of, *B:* 64, 68
as telegraph operator, *B:* 62–65
work habits of, *B:* 64–65
Edison Trust
B: 68
Education
of African Americans, *A:* 161–64
public, *A:* 124
The Education of Henry Adams
***PS:* 61–70**
awarding of Pulitzer Prize for, *PS:* 69

excerpt from *The Education of Henry Adams* (Adams), ***PS:*** 67–68
private publication of, ***PS:*** 69
Efficiency management
A: 200–1
Eight Hours
***PS:* 172–80**
song lyrics of, ***PS:*** 176–78
Eight-hour workday
A: 136
demand for, ***PS:*** 173
movement for, ***PS:*** 174
workers on strike for, ***PS:*** 173 (ill.)
Election(s)
of 1800, ***PS:*** 19
of 1892, ***B:*** 142
of 1896, ***B:*** 140–41, 142
of 1912, ***A:*** 191–92; ***B:*** 116
of 1924, ***B:*** 117–18, 118 (ill.)
of 1932, ***B:*** 119
Electricity, advances in
A: 113
Electromagnetism
B: 63
Electronic Numerical Integrator and Calculator (ENIAC)
A: 212–13, 213 (ill.)
Ellis Island, conditions at
B: 126
Emancipation Proclamation (1863)
B: 176
Emerson, Ralph Waldo, founding of *Atlantic Monthly* by
PS: 195
Engels, Friedrich
A: 143
B: 102, 103, 103 (ill.)
England
exports to United States, ***A:*** 8–9, 14
Industrial Revolution in, ***A:*** 2–6
iron and steel industries in, ***A:*** 4–5
laws preventing export of textile manufacturing machinery, ***B:*** 210–11
living conditions of industrial workers in, ***PS:*** 4 (ill.)
population growth in, ***A:*** 3; ***PS:*** 5
restrictions on United States industry, ***A:*** 10
social changes in, ***A:*** 6–7
textile industry in, ***A:*** 3–4
Enlightenment
PS: 89
Erie Canal
PS: 50 (ill.), 52 (ill.)
celebration on opening of, ***PS:*** 51–52
construction of, ***A:*** 19–20; ***PS:*** 50–51, 53
description of, ***PS:*** 51
impact on economy, ***PS:*** 52–53
transformation of, ***PS:*** 58
vessels used on, ***PS:*** 53–54
Erie Railroad
A: 74 (ill.)
B: 240
PS: 66, 112
stock in, ***A:*** 74–76
Erie War
A: 74–76, 75 (ill.)
B: 240
Espionage Act (1917)
B: 58
Evans, Oliver
A: 32 (ill.)
PS: 28
automated flour mills of, ***A:*** 32–33
Everybody's (magazine)
B: 228
Executive Order 8802
B: 190
Experimental Researches in Electricity and Magnetism (Faraday)
B: 63
Exxon
B: 203

F

Fabian Socialist movement
B: 8
Factories
A: 42, 43 (ill.), 44–45
defined, ***A:*** 4
effect on class system, ***A:*** 9
women workers in, ***A:*** 48, 49, 50, 118 (ill.), 125–26
working conditions in, ***A:*** 42, 44, 50, 120–21
Factory Act (1893)
B: 105
Factory Girls Association
PS: 34
Fair Employment Act
B: 190
Fair Labor Standards Act
A: 125, 195
B: 107, 126
PS: 179
Fall, Albert B.
B: 117
Fall River, Massachusetts, immigrants in
A: 105
Faraday, Michael
B: 63
Farley, Harriet
PS: 41, 42
Farmers' Alliance
A: 178–79
B: 138, 139, 177
Farming. *See also* Agriculture
commercial and mechanized, ***A:*** 35–39
high costs of, ***A:*** 177–78
impact of railroads on, in Old Northwest, ***A:*** 167–69
reaper in, ***A:*** 37–38
steel plow in, ***A:*** 38–39
Fascism
B: 188
Federal Antitrust Legislation, *PS:* 148–59
excerpt from The Interstate Commerce Act of 1887, ***PS:*** 154–56
excerpt from the Sherman Antitrust Act of 1890, ***PS:*** 156–57
Federal Aviation Agency (FAA)
A: 211
Federal Commission on the Conservation of Natural Resources
A: 190
Federal Farm Loan Act
B: 116
Federal Reserve Act (1913)
B: 172–73
Federal Reserve System (FED)
B: 116

Federal Steel
A: 95
B: 36
Federal Tariff Commission
B: 231
Federal Trade Commission (FTC)
A: 193
Federalist Papers, The
PS: 12
Federalist Party
PS: 7, 18
Federated Colored Women's Clubs of Michigan
B: 160
Federation of Organized Trades and Labor Unions
A: 141, 144, 145
PS: 174, 175
Ferguson, Washington
B: 244
Field System (Gilbreth)
B: 92
Fifteenth Amendment
B: 180
Filament manufacturing process
B: 132
Financial panic (1907)
B: 171, 175
Firearms manufacturing
A: 34
Fish, Stuyvesant
PS: 95
Fisk, James
A: 64, 66, 74–76, 74 (ill.)
B: 240
PS: 66
Fitch, John
A: 18, 33
***B:* 71–78**, 72 (ill.)
PS: 27, 28 (ill.)
death of, *B:* 77
early life and work, *B:* 71–74
settlement of, in Kentucky, *B:* 77–78
work on steamboats, *B:* 74–77, 75 (ill.), 237
Fitch, Lucy Roberts
B: 73
Flagler, Henry
B: 198, 201
PS: 114–15, 115 (ill.)
Flanders, Walter E.
B: 84–85
Flatboats
A: 17
Fleming, J. Ambrose
B: 69
Flour mills, Oliver Evans's automated
A: 32–33
Flower, James
B: 81
Flying shuttle
A: 4
B: 209
Folkways (Sumner)
PS: 93
Ford, Clara Bryant
B: 81, 88
Ford, Edsel
B: 87, 88
death of, *B:* 88
Ford, Henry
***B:* 79–88,** 80 (ill.)
control of Ford Motor Company, *B:* 86
death of, *B:* 88
early life of, *B:* 79–81
establishment of Greenfield Village, *B:* 69–70, 87
family of, *B:* 87
influence of, *B:* 85–86
interest in automobile industry, *B:* 81
introduction of Model A by, *B:* 84–85
invention of quadricycle, *B:* 82–83
marriage of, *B:* 81
mass production and, *A:* 201–4
maximum-efficiency concept and, *B:* 79, 84–85
memoirs of, *B:* 80
opposition to labor unions, *B:* 88
production methods of, *B:* 84–85
Rouge plant and, *B:* 86–88, 87 (ill.)
Taylorism and, *B:* 231
World War I and, *B:* 85–86
Ford, Henry, II
B: 88
Ford Motor Company
A: 198 (ill.), 202, 202 (ill.)
B: 79, 83
control of, *B:* 86
Highland Park factory of, *B:* 85
incorporation of, *B:* 83
making changes at, *A:* 204
Model A, *A:* 204; *B:* 84
Model B, *B:* 84
Model N, *B:* 84
Model T, *A:* 202 (ill.), 203, 204; *B:* 84–85
production methods at, *B:* 84–85
Rouge plant, *B:* 86–88, 87 (ill.)
working at, *A:* 203–4
Foreclosure
A: 177
Foreign Miner's Tax (1852)
PS: 72–73
Formation of a Deaf Variety of the Human Race, The (Bell)
B: 27
Forten, James
B: 179
Fourteenth Amendment
A: 193, 194
PS: 82
Franklin, Benjamin
PS: 27
political cartoons of, *PS:* 137
Franklin stove
PS: 27
Frauds, Erie War
A: 74–76
Free market competition
PS: 149
Free silver, as campaign issue in 1896
B: 140–41
Frick, Henry Clay
A: 92–93, 147–48
B: 34, 34 (ill.), 35
Fulton, Robert
A: 18
B: 71, 78, 236, 237

G

Garfield, James A.
B: 27
Garment industry
A: 127
women workers in, *PS:* 162–64, 162 (ill.)
Garrison, Cornelius K.
B: 239

Garrison, William Lloyd
B: 130
Garvey, Marcus
B: 185–86
Gary, Elbert H.
B: 231–32
Gas lamps
B: 67
Gates, Frederick T.
B: 205
Gaugers
A: 72
General Education Board
B: 200, 205
General Electric Company
B: 68, 95, 133, 134, 232
General Managers' Association (GMA)
A: 145
B: 53–54
General Motors (GM)
A: 204
B: 83
German immigrants
PS: 82
GI Bills of Rights
A: 211
Gibbons, Thomas
B: 237–38
Gibbons v. Ogden
B: 237
Gilbreth, Anne
B: 92
Gilbreth, Frank
***B:* 89–98,** 90 (ill.)
ambitions of, *B:* 91
death of, *B:* 97
early life of, *B:* 90–91, 92
family of, *B:* 94, 97 (ill.)
household management system of, *B:* 96–99
industrial management and, *B:* 93–94
interest in Taylorism, *B:* 93–94
one best way theory and, *B:* 91, 92
patents of, *B:* 91
philosophy of, *B:* 92–93
work style of, *B:* 91
work with war veterans, *B:* 95–96
writing skills of, *B:* 92
Gilbreth, Frank, Jr.
B: 96
Gilbreth, Jane
B: 92
Gilbreth, Lillian Moller
***B:* 89–98,** 90 (ill.)
death of, *B:* 98
early life of, *B:* 92
family of, *B:* 94
founding of Motion Study Institute, *B:* 97
industrial psychology and, *B:* 93
interest in Taylorism, *B:* 93–94
philosophy of, *B:* 92–93
work on women's work, *B:* 97–98
work with disabled, *B:* 98
work with war veterans, *B:* 95–96
writing skills of, *B:* 92
Gilbreth, Mary
B: 94
Gilded Age
A: 56–67, 84, 87, 94, 108, 114, 122, 197
PS: 61, 84, 136, 181
concentration of wealth during, *PS:* 95
political cartoons in, *PS:* 137–38
wealthy and business classes during, *B:* 16–17
Gilman, Charlotte Perkins
B: 8
Gladden, Washington
A: 97 (ill.)
Glass industry
A: 194 (ill.)
Glidden, Joseph
A: 173, 174 (ill.)
Gold and Stock Telegraphic Company
B: 65
Gold mines, work of Chinese in
B: 43–44
Gold Rush (1848)
A: 106
PS: 72
Gompers, Samuel
A: 144
B: 55
Gospel of wealth
A: 94–95
Gould, Jay
A: 64, 66, 74–76
B: 166, 240, 240 (ill.)
PS: 65, 65 (ill.), 66–67, 69, 112
Grady, Henry W.
A: 156, 156 (ill.)
Grain trade
A: 168–69
Grand Canyon
A: 190
Grand Trunk Railway
A: 88
B: 62
Grange
B: 112
PS: 150, 151 (ill.)
agriculture and, *A:* 175–77, 176 (ill.)
Granger Laws
A: 177
PS: 150
Grant, Ulysses S.
PS: 77
Corbin as brother-in-law to, *A:* 66
scandals under, *PS:* 63
Gray, Elisha
B: 24, 27, 131
Grayson, David
B: 55
Great American Desert
A: 170
Great Depression (1929–41)
A: 206–7
B: 119
PS: 178
Great Lakes
A: 20
B: 74
PS: 53, 59
Great Migration
B: 251
Great Northern Railroad
A: 187–88
B: 170
Great Plains
A: 38, 166
end of open range and, *A:* 173–75
extermination of buffalo on, *A:* 170–71
homesteaders in, *A:* 169–70
Great Strikes of 1877
A: 139–40
Great Train Robbery, The (film)
B: 68

A = Development of the Industrial U.S.: Almanac—
B = Development of the Industrial U.S.: Biographies

Green Bay, Wisconsin, living conditions in
B: 114
Green, Lucille
B: 185
Greene, Catharine Littlefield
PS: 21, 23
Greene, Nathanael
PS: 22
Greener, Richard
B: 134
Greenfield Village Museum
B: 69–70, 87
Grosse Pointe, Michigan
B: 83
Guns, Whitney's work on
PS: 26–27

H

Hale, Sarah
A: 50
Half-Century Exposition of Freedmen's Progress
B: 160
Hall Carbine Affair
B: 165
Hall, John
A: 32
Hamilton, Alexander
B: 149
PS: 10–20, 14 (ill.)
as author of *The Federalist Papers*, *PS:* 12
as champion of industry, *PS:* 12–14
as delegate to Constitutional Convention (1787), *PS:* 12
duel with Burr, *PS:* 19
economic depression and, *A:* 9
education of, *PS:* 10
employment of women and children and, *PS:* 11 (ill.)
excerpt from *Congressional Report on Manufacturers* by, *PS:* 13, 15–18
as first secretary of the treasury, *PS:* 12
as member of Washington's military staff, *PS:* 11
personality of, *PS:* 19
pro-manufacturing vision of, *A:* 10
as secretary of the treasury, *PS:* 6–7, 10
on stimulating economy, *PS:* 18
support for manufacturing, *PS:* 7
support for patents, *PS:* 27
Hammer & Schwarz (law firm)
B: 134
Hampton Normal and Agricultural Institute
A: 161
B: 246–47
Harding, Warren G.
release of Debs by, *B:* 59
Teapot Dome scandal and, *B:* 117
Unemployment Conference and, *B:* 231
Hargreaves, James
A: 4
B: 209
Harlem Railroad
A: 75
Harmonic telegraph
B: 24, 25
Harper's Monthly (magazine)
A: 77
Harper's Weekly (magazine)
A: 185
PS: 137, 145
Harriman, Edward H.
A: 187–88
B: 170
Harris (Triangle Shirtwaist Factory owner)
PS: 168
Harrison, Benjamin, antitrust policy under
A: 99
Hartford, Connecticut, growth of
A: 103
Hawthorne, Nathaniel
PS: 49–60, 54 (ill.)
excerpt from "The Canal Boat" by, *PS:* 54–57
founding of *Atlantic Monthly* by, *PS:* 195
Hayes, Rutherford B.
election of, *B:* 178
Great Strikes of 1877 and, *A:* 139
Reconstruction Era and, *A:* 156
Haymarket Square Riot
A: 141–43, 142 (ill.)
hanging of leaders, *PS:* 175 (ill.)
trial for leaders of, *PS:* 203–4
Haywood, William "Big Bill"
A: 148
Health insurance, nonexistence of
A: 117
Helmholtz, Hermann von
B: 23
Henry, Joseph
A: 25
Henry Street Settlement
B: 134
Hershey, Pennsylvania, growth of
A: 103
Hill, James J.
A: 64, 187–88
B: 170
Hine, Lewis
A: 123
PS: 107
Historical materialism
A: 143
The History of Standard Oil
***PS:* 124–35**
excerpt from *The History of the Standard Oil Company* (Tarbell), *PS:* 130–33
rank of, as number 5 on list of best one hundred works of twentieth-century American journalism, *PS:* 134
History of the Standard Oil Company, The (Tarbell)
A: 185–86
B: 203, 230
Holburn Viaduct
B: 68
Holmes, Oliver Wendell
PS: 195
Home Insurance Company Building
A: 115
B: 34–35
Home-Maker and Her Job, The (Gilbreth)
B: 97–98
Homestead Act (1862)
A: 60, 169

Homestead Steel Works
A: 93 (ill.)
B: 34
sale to Morgan, *B:* 36
strike at, *A:* 92–93, 146–48; *B:* 35–36; *PS:* 139
Homesteaders, in Great Plains
A: 169–70
Hoover, Herbert
B: 70
as secretary of commerce, *A:* 205
Hopkins, Mark
A: 71
Hopper boy
A: 32, 33
Horizontal expansion
A: 87
PS: 118
Horse-drawn street railcar
A: 104, 104 (ill.)
Horseless carriage
B: 79
Hotel Messenger (magazine)
B: 185
Household management system
B: 96–99
How the Other Half Lives
A: 111–12
***PS:* 97–108**
excerpt from *How the Other Half Lives: Studies Among the Tenements of New York* (Riis), *PS:* 102–5
publication of, and friendship with T. Roosevelt, *PS:* 105
Howe, Elias
A: 52
Howells, William Cooper
PS: 194
Howells, William Dean
PS: 194–205, 198 (ill.)
devotion of, to American literature, *PS:* 196
early life of, *PS:* 194–95
as editor of *Atlantic Monthly*, *PS:* 195–96
excerpt from *The Rise of Silas Lapham* by, *PS:* 199–203
memoirs of, *PS:* 194–95
philosophy in writing of, *PS:* 197
Hubbard, Gardiner G.
B: 24, 26
Hubbard, Mabel G.
B: 26
Hudson River Association
B: 238
Hudson River Railroad
B: 240
Hull, Charles J.
B: 5
Hull House
A: 112
B: 4 (ill.), 7, 102, 104, 124
founding of, *B:* 1, 3–5, 100, 120, 121–22, 215, 218, 220
historic firsts, *B:* 7
Kelley at, *B:* 100, 102
Lathrop's support for, *B:* 120, 126–27
renovation of, *B:* 6
services offered at, *B:* 1, 6–7, 8
visitors to, *B:* 7–8
Hull-House Maps and Papers: A Presentation of Nationalities and Wages in a Congested District of Chicago, Together with Comments and Essays on Problems Growing Out of the Social Conditions
B: 105, 123–24, 219
Huntington, Collis P.
A: 64, 71
Hypatia Club
B: 138

I

ICC Sunset Act (1995)
PS: 157
"I Have a Dream" speech (King, Jr.)
B: 191
Illinois Board of Public Charities, Lathrop on
B: 122–23, 124
Illinois Bureau of Labor Statistics
B: 104
Illinois Factory Act (1893)
A: 123
B: 106
Illinois League of Women Voters
B: 126
Immigrants
Chinese, *A:* 73–74, 105–6; *PS:* 71–76, 72 (ill), 80
in cities, *A:* 105, 126–27
city life of, *PS:* 101, 102
education of, *A:* 112
German, *PS:* 82
Irish, *A:* 73; *PS:* 46–47, 82
new, *A:* 105, 120
old, *A:* 105, 120
in workforce, *A:* 126–27
Immigration
A: 105–6
legislation on, *A:* 61–62
In As Much Circle of King's Daughters and Sons Club
B: 160
Incandescent Electric Lighting (Latimer)
B: 133
Incandescent lamp
A: 113, 114 (ill.)
Incandescent light bulb
B: 60, 67–68
Income tax
A: 85
Incorporation
A: 22
Industrial age, workers in
A: 117–31
Industrial management
B: 89
application to homes, *B:* 96–99
Frank Gilbreth's interest in, *B:* 93–94
Industrial psychology, Lillian Gilbreth's interest in
B: 93–94
Industrial Revolution
B: 19
in England, *A:* 2–6; *PS:* 1–2
in United States, *A:* 1; *PS:* 4, 49
Industrial workers, living conditions of, in England
PS: 4 (ill.)
Industrial Workers of the World (IWW)
A: 148, 149
demonstration by, *A:* 134 (ill.)
Industrialists, abuse of workers by
PS: 1, 2 (ill.)
Industrialization
benefits of, *A:* 65–67
development of, in United States, *A:* 7–8

effect of, on farming and ranching in West, **A:** 166–80
foundations of, **A:** 56
impact of Civil War on, **A:** 63
key factors of, **A:** 63–64
second wave of, **A:** 57
spread of, across United States, **PS:** 71
in twentieth century, **A:** 197–216

Industries
after World War I, **A:** 205
airline, **A:** 210–11, 211 (ill.)
boot, **A:** 52–55, 54 (ill.)
cattle, **A:** 172–75
clothing, **A:** 50–51
garment, **A:** 127
glass, **A:** 194 (ill.)
infant, **A:** 10
iron, **A:** 4–5
meatpacking, **A:** 88, 163, 186–87
oil, **A:** 63
shoe, **A:** 52–55, 54 (ill.)
steel, **A:** 4–5
textile, **A:** 3–4, 10, 43 (ill.), 45–47
tobacco, **A:** 157–59

Infant mortality rates, Lathrop's interest in reducing
B: 125

Ingalls, John J.
B: 139–40

Injunction
A: 146
B: 56

Interchangeable parts
A: 34
PS: 27
production of, **A:** 30–31

Intercollegiate Socialist Society
B: 107

Internal-combustion engine
B: 82

International Brotherhood of Sleeping Car Porters
B: 190, 192

International Business Machines (IBM)
A: 213–14

International Centennial Exhibition (Philadelphia, PA)
B: 26

International Congress of Women
B: 9

International Labor Day
PS: 175

International Ladies Garment Workers Union (ILGWU)
B: 220
formation of, **PS:** 164
founding of Health Center, **PS:** 169
position of Pauline Newman with, **PS:** 168–69
Triangle employees as members of, **PS:** 164–65

International Typographical Union
A: 134–35

International Workers Day, celebration of
PS: 179–80

Interstate Commerce Act (1887)
A: 97–98, 99, 184
PS: 149, 153
excerpt from, **PS:** 154–56
vague wording of, **PS:** 154

Interstate Commerce Commission (ICC)
A: 184, 210
B: 93
PS: 153
creation of, **PS:** 157

Interstate Commerce Railway Association
B: 166–67

Interstate commerce, regulation of
A: 98
PS: 152–54

Inventions, agriculture and
A: 169–71

Iowa State College of Agriculture and Mechanic Arts
B: 248

"Ireland and Irishmen" (Lease)
B: 138

Irish immigrants
B: 44
PS: 82
in construction of Central Pacific **A:** 73
life of, **PS:** 46–47

Iron
English production of, **A:** 4–5
U.S. production of, prior to 1865, **A:** 39

J

Jackson, Andrew
B: 214

James, Henry
PS: 196

Japan, invasion of China by
PS: 81

Jay, John, as author of *The Federalist Papers*
PS: 12

Jefferson, Thomas
A: 9 (ill.)
PS: 1–8, 8 (ill.)
administration of, **PS:** 18
as author of Declaration of Independence (1776), **PS:** 3
decision not to seek patents, **PS:** 27
as delegate to Continental Congress, **PS:** 3
education of, **PS:** 3
in election of 1800, **PS:** 19
excerpt from *Notes on the State of Virginia* by, **PS:** 5–6
as governor of Virginia, **PS:** 3
on industry, **PS:** 1–4
as leader of Democratic-Republicans, **PS:** 7–8
opportunities of, **B:** 78
pro-agricultural vision of, **A:** 9
reputation as scholar, **PS:** 3
as secretary of state, **A:** 9, 33; **B:** 76; **PS:** 6–7, 23, 25
slavery and, **PS:** 4, 8
support for republicanism, **PS:** 1
as Virginia legislator, **PS:** 3

Jennings, Thomas L.
B: 178

Jersey Standard
B: 203

Jet propulsion
A: 18

Jewish conspiracy
B: 86

Jim Crow laws
A: 163
B: 250

Job-related injuries, Debs position on
B: 52
John Bull (train)
A: 24
Joint-stock company
B: 147–50
Jones, Jesse Henry
PS: 174, 176
Jones, Mary "Mother,"
A: 148
Journal (Wichita) (newspaper)
B: 138
Journalism, muckrakers and
A: 97, 185–87
Judah, Theodore Dehone
A: 71, 74
Jungle, The (Sinclair)
A: 186–87
B: 228
Juvenile offenders, Lathrop's work with
B: 124–25

K

Kahn, Albert
B: 84
Kansas, antitrust legislation in
A: 98
PS: 152
Kansas City, Kansas
A: 178
Kansas Pacific Railroad
A: 170–73
Kay, John
A: 4
B: 209
Kearney, Denis
PS: 77, 77 (ill.)
Keating-Owen Child Labor Act
A: 195
B: 116
Keelboats
A: 17
Kelley, Florence
A: 123
B: **100–7**, 101 (ill.)
background and education, *B:* 100–3
child labor and, *B:* 100, 104
death of, *B:* 107
establishment of Children's Bureau and, *B:* 125
health problems of, *B:* 101–2
Hull House and, *B:* 100, 102, 220
interest in consumer action, *B:* 106
Lathrop's inclusion in book written by, *B:* 123
legacy of, *B:* 106–7
marriage of, *B:* 102, 104
maternity care and, *B:* 106–7
reforms of, in Chicago, *B:* 104–6
as translator, *B:* 102, 104
work at Illinois Bureau of Labor Statistics, *B:* 104–6
Kelley, Oliver Hudson
A: 175
Kelley, William Darrah
B: 100
Kern-McGillicuddy Act (1916)
A: 196
B: 116
Kerosene
A: 89
lamps using, *A:* 113
Keynes, John Maynard
PS: 179
Keystone Bridge Company
B: 33
Kindergarten
A: 112
King, Charles B.
B: 82
King, Martin Luther, Jr.
B: 191
"I Have a Dream" speech, *B:* 182
King's College
PS: 10
Kirkland School for Girls
B: 217
Knights of Labor
A: 136–37, 143, 149
under Powderly, *A:* 140
Kuangtung Province
B: 41

L

La Follette, Belle Case
B: 111, 112
La Follette, Bob, Jr.
B: 112, 119
La Follette, Josiah
B: 109–10
La Follette, Mary
B: 112
La Follette, Philip
B: 112, 119
La Follette, Robert M.
B: **109–19**, 110 (ill.)
Abraham Lincoln and, *B:* 110
background and early career, *B:* 109–11
as candidate for president, *B:* 117–19, 118 (ill.)
founding of Progressive Party by, *B:* 109, 112–13
as governor of Wisconsin, *B:* 113, 114–15
legacy of, *B:* 116, 119
political interests of, *B:* 111
popular support for, *B:* 114–15
Progressive agenda of, *B:* 112–13
in the Senate, *B:* 109, 115–16
World War I and, *B:* 116–17
La Follette's Magazine
B: 112, 116
Labor Day
celebration of *PS:* 180
history of, *A:* 145
parade on, *A:* 145 (ill.)
Labor movement. *See also* Labor unions
A: 133–50
African Americans and, *A:* 149–50; *B:* 189
American Federation of Labor in, *A:* 144, 145, 146
Depression of 1873 and, *A:* 137–39
eight-hour day in, *A:* 136
Ellen Gates Starr in, *B:* 219–21
Federation of Organized Trades and Labor Unions in, *A:* 141, 144, 145
Ford's opposition to unions, *B:* 88
Great Strikes of 1877 in, *A:* 139–40
Haymarket Square Riot in, *A:* 141–43, 142 (ill.)
Homestead Strike in, *A:* 92–93, 146–48

Industrial Workers of the World (IWW) in, *A:* 148, 149
Knights of Labor in, *A:* 136–37, 140, 143, 149
National Labor Union in, *A:* 136, 149
Pullman strike in, *A:* 144–46
rise and fall of unions in twentieth century, *A:* 150
Tarbell's interest in, *B:* 231–32
Theodore Roosevelt and, *A:* 189, 191
United Mine Workers in, *A:* 144, 149, 150, 191
work stoppages in, *A:* 54–55
Labor unions. *See also* Labor movement; *specific*
African American, *A:* 149–50
defined, *A:* 133
history of U.S., *A:* 134–35
rise and fall of, in twentieth century, *A:* 150
women in, *A:* 50; *PS:* 163
Labor, U.S. Department of, establishment of
A: 191
B: 117
Laboratory Volta Bureau for the Increase and Diffusion of Knowledge Relating to the Deaf
B: 27
LaGuardia, Fiorello
B: 187
Laid-off workers
A: 215
Laissez-faire policies
A: 62–63, 85, 122, 131, 182
PS: 86, 117, 149
Lake Ontario
PS: 59
Lake Shore and Michigan Railroad
B: 241
Lake Superior
PS: 59
Land advertisement
A: 168 (ill.)
Lasting Machine
A: 53
Lathrop, Adeline
B: 121
Lathrop, Julia C.
A: 125
***B:* 120–27,** 121 (ill.)
death of, *B:* 127
as director of Children's Bureau, *B:* 120, 125–26
early life and education of, *B:* 120–22
efforts to end child labor, *B:* 126
interest in reducing infant mortality rates, *B:* 125
public service of, *B:* 122–24
support for Hull House, *B:* 120, 126–27
work with juvenile offenders, *B:* 124–25
Lathrop, William
B: 120
Latimer, Emma Jeannette
B: 134
Latimer, George
B: 128–29
Latimer Lamp
B: 133
Latimer, Lewis H.
***B:* 128–34,** 129 (ill.)
career achievements of, *B:* 128, 133–34
death of, *B:* 134
as draftsman, *B:* 130, 131
early life of, *B:* 128–30
family of, *B:* 131
patents of, *B:* 128, 132
prejudice against, *B:* 133
work on light bulb, *B:* 132–33
work with Alexander Graham Bell, *B:* 130–32
Latimer, Louise
B: 134
Latimer, Mary
B: 131
Latimer, Rebecca
B: 128–29, 130
Lawrence, Massachusetts, immigrants in
A: 105
Le Baron, William
A: 115
Leadville, Nevada
A: 178
League of Nations, Child Welfare Committee
B: 126
Lease, Charles L.
B: 138
Lease, Mary Elizabeth
***B:* 136–43,** 137 (ill.)
death of, *B:* 143
early life of, *B:* 136–38
legacy of, *B:* 143
marriage of, *B:* 138
oratorical skills of, *B:* 136, 138–40
in Populist movement, *B:* 140–42
Letter (magazine)
B: 232
Letters to Michael and Hugh
***PS:* 161–71**
excerpt from Letters to Michael and Hugh Owens (Newman), *PS:* 165–67
Leveraged buyout
B: 241
Lewelling, Lorenzo
B: 142
Liberator (newspaper)
B: 130
Life and Labour of the People of London (Booth)
B: 105
Liggett and Myers
A: 159
Light, advances in
A: 113
Light bulbs, Latimer's work on
B: 132–33
Light in Dark Places (Murray)
B: 180
Lily, The (magazine)
PS: 47
Lincoln, Abraham
PS: 62, 127
Emancipation Proclamation by, *B:* 245
Ida Tarbell's biography of, *A:* 185; *B:* 227
Jane Addams and, *B:* 3
La Follette and, *B:* 110
transcontinental railroad and, *A:* 60
transport of, for funeral, *A:* 81
Lincoln miller
A: 35
Lindbergh, Charles A.
A: 210

Line boats
PS: 53
List of Four Hundred
B: 13–15, 16, 17
Livingston, Robert
B: 77–78, 236, 236 (ill.)
Lloyd, Henry Demarest
A: 96–97, 96 (ill.)
B: 104, 201, 228
PS: 94, 127
as editor of *Atlantic Monthly, PS:* 115–16
Lochner v. New York
A: 194
Lockport, New York
PS: 53
Lodge, Henry Cabot
PS: 69
London, Crystal Palace Exhibition in
A: 39–40, 40 (ill.)
London, Jack
B: 107
London, population of
PS: 5
Loom and Spindle
***PS:* 30–38**
excerpt from *Loom and Spindle, or, Life among the Early Mill Girls* (Robinson), *PS:* 34–36
Looms
A: 4
power, *A:* 45–46, 47
Lorillard, P., Company
A: 159
Louis XVI (King of France)
B: 77
Louisville, Kentucky, settlement of
A: 19
Lowell Female Labor Reform Association (LFLRA)
A: 50
PS: 47
Lowell, Francis Cabot
A: 46 (ill.), 50
***B:* 144–52**, 145 (ill.)
PS: 30, 32
death of, *B:* 150–51
early work in shipping industry, *B:* 144–46
establishment of textile industry, *A:* 45–47
expansion of Lowell mills and, *B:* 151–52
legacy of, *B:* 144
main competitor to Samuel Slater, *B:* 213
organization of Boston Manufacturing Company, *B:* 148–49
studying of textile technology in England, *B:* 146–47
Lowell girls
B: 150–51
PS: 30–32, 31 (ill.)
free time of, *PS:* 33, 41
opportunities for, *PS:* 38
Lowell, Hannah Jackson
B: 145
Lowell, James Russell, founding of *Atlantic Monthly* by
PS: 195
Lowell, John
B: 144
Lowell, Massachusetts, Irish immigrants in
PS: 46–47
Lowell mills
A: 47
housing for workers in, *PS:* 31–32, 37
strikes at, *PS:* 34
success of, *A:* 49
wages for workers, *PS:* 34
women workers in, *A:* 48, 49; *PS:* 30–32, 31 (ill.), 39
working conditions in, *PS:* 33–34, 37, 39, 41
The Lowell Offering
***PS:* 30–48**, 40 (ill.)
excerpt from "A Second Peep at Factory Life," article in, *PS:* 43–46
merits of, as literary production, *PS:* 42–43
Lowell Offering (journal)
A: 49, 49 (ill.)
Lowell System
B: 150
Lung diseases
A: 121–22
Lydian Association of Detroit
B: 160
Lynchings
A: 163
Lynn, Massachusetts
growth of, *A:* 103
Shoe City in, *A:* 54, 54 (ill.)
strike in, *A:* 54–55

M

MacDonald, James Ramsay, visits by, to Hull House
B: 7–8
Machine makers
PS: 14
Machine shop, apprentices in
A: 29 (ill.)
Macy's
A: 115
Madison, James
as author of *The Federalist Papers, PS:* 12
support for patents, *PS:* 27
Making of an American (Riis)
PS: 105
Malcomson, Alexander Y.
B: 83, 84
Manchester, England, Lowell's study of textile technology in
B: 146–47
Mann, Horace
A: 124
Mantle clock
A: 34
Manufacturing, Hamilton's views on
A: 10
March on Washington for Jobs and Freedom (1963)
B: 182, 190–92
March on Washington Movement (1941)
B: 188–90
Marshall Field's
A: 115
B: 104
Martin, Pierre Émile
A: 92
Marx, Karl
A: 143
B: 102, 103
Mass production
PS: 14, 27
adaptation to clock making, *A:* 34

in computer age, ***A:*** 214–15
Henry Ford and, ***A:*** 201–4
Massachusetts in the Woman Suffrage Movement (Robinson)
PS: 37
Maternity care, Kelley's interest in
B: 106–7
Matzeliger, Jan Ernst
A: 53
Maxim, Hiram S.
B: 131, 132, 133
Maximum-efficiency concept, Ford's interest in
B: 84–85
May Day, celebration of
PS: 179–80
McAllister, Ward
B: 13–15, 14 (ill.), 19
McClure, Samuel S.
A: 185–86
B: 226, 230
PS: 127, 127 (ill.), 128
McClure's (magazine)
A: 185–86
B: 55, 202, 228
circulation of, ***PS:*** 127, 128
Standard Oil exposé in, ***B:*** 227–30
Tarbell at, ***B:*** 226–80
Tarbell's articles in, ***PS:*** 127–28
McCormick, Cyrus
A: 171
McCormick Harvester Company
A: 141
strike at, ***A:*** 141–42; ***PS:*** 174–75, 203
McCormick reaper
A: 37–38
McCoy, Elijah
***B:* 154–60**, 155 (ill.)
development of automatic engine lubricator, ***B:*** 156–58, 157 (ill.)
early life of, ***B:*** 154–56
founding of Elijah McCoy Manufacturing Company by, ***B:*** 159
illness and death of, ***B:*** 159
patents of, ***B:*** 154, 159
prejudice against, ***B:*** 158
McCoy, Elijah, Manufacturing Company
B: 159
McCoy, Joseph G.
A: 172–73
McCoy, Mary Delaney
B: 159
McCoy, Mary Eleanora
B: 160
McKinley, William
antitrust policy under, ***A:*** 99
assassination of, ***A:*** 187, ***B:*** 115
in election of 1896, ***A:*** 180, ***B:*** 141, 142
McParlan, James
A: 139
Meat Inspection Act
A: 187
Meatpacking industry
in Chicago, ***A:*** 88, 163
conditions in, ***A:*** 88
investigation of, ***A:*** 186–87
Mechanical reapers
A: 171
Mechanicians
A: 28
Mechanization of farming
A: 35–39
Mellon, Andrew W.
B: 70
Memorial of the Chinese Six Companies
***PS:* 71–83**
text of "Memorial of the Chinese Six Companies to U.S. Grant, President of the United States," ***PS:*** 78–80
Memphis, Tennessee, growth of
A: 103
Menlo Park, New Jersey
B: 65
laboratory in, ***B:*** 66 (ill.)
Mercantile
A: 7–8
Mergers
PS: 151
Messenger, The (magazine)
B: 185
Metalworking
A: 10
Metropolitan Museum of Art
A: 94
B: 174, 200
Metropolitan Opera
B: 242
Michigan Central Railroad
A: 167
B: 156–58, 159, 241
Michigan Salt Association
A: 87
PS: 118
Michigan Southern
A: 167
Michigan State Association of Colored Women
B: 160
Microsoft
PS: 158–59
Migration
of African Americans, ***A:*** 107–8, 163
from farm to cities, ***A:*** 106–8
Miller, Phineas
PS: 22, 24
Milwaukee Free Press (newspaper)
B: 114
Milwaukee Sentinel (newspaper)
B: 114
Milwaukee, Wisconsin
growth of, ***A:*** 103
immigrants in, ***A:*** 105
living conditions in, ***B:*** 114
Minimum wage
A: 195
Mississippi River, early traffic on
A: 17
Mitchell, John
A: 189 (ill.), 191
Mobil
B: 203
Model A automobiles
A: 204
Model T automobiles
A: 202 (ill.), 203, 204; ***B:*** 79
Molders Union
A: 136
Molly Maguires
A: 138–39, 138 (ill.)
Monopolies
A: 64, 87, 182
B: 170
PS: 87–88, 118, 142
early response to, ***A:*** 96–97
Standard Oil as, ***B:*** 198–200, 223, 228–29

Mont-Saint-Michel and Chartres (Adams)
PS: 63–64
Montgomery Ward and Company
A: 176
Montreal
PS: 59
Moody, Paul
B: 146–47
Morgan, Amelia Sturges
B: 164
Morgan, Anne
B: 164
Morgan, Charles
B: 239
Morgan, Frances Tracy
B: 164
Morgan, J. P.
A: 64, 82, 98, 188
B: 162–75, 163 (ill.)
PS: 148, 152
Andrew Carnegie and, **B:** 30, 169
death of, **B:** 174
at Duncan, Sherman & Company, **B:** 164
Edison Electric Light Company and, **B:** 67
education of, **B:** 163–64
family of, **B:** 164
financial empire of, **B:** 162, 167
founding of own firm, **B:** 165
government and, **B:** 171
influence on American economy, **B:** 162–63
Morganization and, **A:** 157
philanthropy of, **A:** 94, **B:** 174
Pujo Money Trust Investigation and, **B:** 172–75
purchase of Carnegie Steel, **PS:** 144–45
as robber baron, **B:** 162
setting up of steel cartel by, **B:** 36
Thomas Edison and, **B:** 169
U.S. Steel and, **A:** 95
wealth of, **PS:** 88
work for railroad industry, **B:** 165–66
Morgan, J. P., & Company
B: 168, 168 (ill.), 172
Morgan, J. P., Jr.
B: 164
Morgan, Juliet Pierpont
B: 163–64
Morgan, Junius Spenser
B: 163, 165
death of, **B:** 168
Morgan, Louisa Juliet
B: 164
Morgan, Pierpont, Library
B: 174
Morganization
A: 82, 157, 188
B: 166–67
Morse code
B: 63
Morse, Samuel F. B.
A: 25, 26 (ill.)
B: 63
PS: 89
Mortgage foreclosures
A: 208
Motion picture industry, Edison's contribution to
B: 68–69
Motion Picture Patents Company (MPPC)
B: 68–69
Motion study experiments
B: 94
Motion Study Institute, founding of
B: 97
Motley, John Lothrop
PS: 64
Muckrakers. *See also* Tarbell, Ida M.
A: 97, 185–87
B: 55, 228–29
Muckraking
PS: 69, 127–29
Mulberry Bend Park
PS: 106
Muller v. Oregon
PS: 178
Munn v. Illinois
PS: 153
Murray, George Washington
B: 176–80
death of, **B:** 180
early life of, **B:** 176
education of, **B:** 176–77
Farmers' Alliance and, **B:** 177
patents of, **B:** 177
politics and, **B:** 177–78, 180
Museum of the City of New York
PS: 106
Muskets, manufacture of
A: 31–32
PS: 26–27
Mussolini, Benito
B: 232
My Friend, Julia Lathrop (Addams)
B: 127
Myers, Isaac
A: 149

N

Nast, Thomas, political cartoons by
PS: 137, 145
Nation (newspaper)
PS: 62–63
National Association for the Advancement of Colored People (NAACP)
B: 160, 251
National Association of Colored Women (NACW)
B: 160
National Bank Acts (1863 and 1864)
A: 61
B: 172
National Cash Register Company (Corning, New York)
A: 103
National Child Labor Committee
A: 123, 195
National Conference of Charities and Corrections
B: 9, 106
National Consumers' League
B: 106
National Farmers' Alliance & Industrial Union
A: 164
National Foundation of Settlements and Neighborhood Centers
B: 9
National Geographic Society
B: 28
National Grange of the Patrons of Husbandry
A: 175–77, 176 (ill.)
National Industrial Recovery Act (1933)
PS: 178–79

A = Development of the Industrial U.S.: Almanac—
B = Development of the Industrial U.S.: Biographies

National Labor Union
A: 136, 149
National Monuments Act (1906)
A: 190
National Progressive Republican League
B: 116
National Road
A: 17
National Simplified Spelling Board
B: 37
National Steel
A: 95
Natural selection
PS: 89
Naturalization Act (1790)
PS: 82
Nebraska, settlement of
A: 59 (ill.)
Negro American Labor Council (NALC)
B: 190
Netscape
PS: 159
New Deal
A: 207–9
New England Butt Company
B: 94
New England Workingmen's Association
PS: 47
New England Yearly Meeting Boarding School
B: 149
New Haven, Connecticut, growth of
A: 103
New Ideas in Business, and Account of Their Practice and Their Effect Upon Men and Profits (Tarbell)
B: 231
New immigrants
A: 105, 120
New Orleans, Louisiana
A: 102, 168
New Orleans (steamboat)
B: 78
New York and Harlem Railroad
B: 239
New York Central and Hudson River Railroad
B: 240–41
New York Central Railroad
A: 79
B: 166, 240
New York City
A: 101 (ill.), 102
Children's Aid Society in, *PS:* 191–92
garment industry in, *A:* 127; *PS:* 162–64, 162 (ill.)
growth of, *A:* 103, 167
homeless children in, *PS:* 183, 184 (ill.)
immigrants in, *A:* 105; *PS:* 101, 102, 161–62, 183
millionaires in, *B:* 10
nouveaux riche in, *B:* 10–11
political machine in, *A:* 110–11
population of, *A:* 7, 103, 108; *PS:* 101
slums of, *A:* 111–12
streetcars in, *A:* 107
sweatshops in, *PS:* 163–64
tenements in, *PS:* 101–2, 161–62
New York Consumers' League
B: 107
New York Society for the Prevention of Cruelty to Children
PS: 192
New York Stock Exchange (NYSE)
A: 65, 65 (ill.), 77, 175
New York Sun, Riis as reporter for
PS: 99–100
New York Tribune, Riis as reporter for
PS: 98–99
New York World (newspaper)
B: 143
Newcomen, Thomas
A: 5
B: 74
Newlands National Reclamation Act (1902)
A: 190
Newman, Pauline M.
PS: 161–70
early life of, *PS:* 161
employment of, at Triangle Shirtwaist Factory, *PS:* 161
excerpt from *Letters to Michael and Hugh [Owens] from P. M. Newman* by, *PS:* 165–67
position with International Ladies' Garment Workers Union (ILGWU), *PS:* 168–69
as speaker at Triangle strikes, *PS:* 165
Newport, Rhode Island
B: 13, 19
News Reporting Telegraph Company
B: 65
Niagara Falls
PS: 53
Niagara Movement
B: 251
Nichols, Joseph V.
B: 132
Nineteenth Amendment
B: 126
Noble Order of the Knights of Labor
A: 136–37
PS: 173–74
Normal Lives for the Disabled (Gilbreth and Yost)
B: 98
Norris, Frank
B: 55
PS: 196
North American Review, Adams as editor of
PS: 63
North, industrial
A: 153–54
North River (steamboat)
B: 78
Northern Alliance
A: 178–79
Northern Pacific Railroad
A: 76, 77, 169, 188
B: 170
Northern Securities Co. v. U.S.
PS: 158
Northern Securities Company
A: 188
Northern Securities Trust Company
B: 170–71
Northrop Aircraft
A: 212
Northwest Territory
B: 74
Northwestern University
A: 94

Notes on the State of Virginia
A: 9
***PS:* 1–9**
excerpt from *Notes on the State of Virginia* (Jefferson), ***PS:*** 5–6
questions posed in, ***PS:*** 3–4
Nouveaux riche
B: 10–11
Novel of Manners in America, The (Tuttleton)
PS: 196–97
Nynex
B: 28

O

Ohio, antitrust legislation in
PS: 152
Ohio River, early traffic on
A: 17
Ohio State Journal
PS: 195
Ohio v. Standard Oil Co. Ohio
PS: 142
Oil industry, creation of
A: 63
Old immigrants
A: 105, 120
Old Northwest
A: 17, 19, 166
PS: 49
impact of railroads on farming in, *A:* 167–69
Old Slater Mill
B: 214
Oliver, James
A: 170–71
Omaha, Nebraska
A: 178
One best way theory
B: 92
Opdyke, George
A: 51
Open range, end of
A: 173–75
Open-hearth furnace process
A: 92
B: 34
Original Steamboat Supported, The (Fitch)
B: 76
Orphan trains
PS: 191–92
Overproduction
A: 175
Owen, Chandler
B: 185

P

Pacific Railroad Act (1862)
A: 71–72
Packet-boats
PS: 52 (ill.), 53–54
Panama Canal
B: 239
Panic
of 1873, *A:* 76–77, 175, 176
of 1893, *A:* 82, 183
Papin, Denis
B: 74
Paris Exhibition of 1900
PS: 64
Paris Peace Conference (1918)
B: 232
Partnerships
B: 147
Patent Act (1790)
PS: 25
Patent Office, U.S.
A: 33
B: 212
PS: 28
creation of, ***PS:*** 25
Patents
A: 28, 33
B: 128
of Bell, ***B:*** 24–26
of Edison, ***B:*** 64, 68
of Gilbreth, Frank, ***B:*** 91
infringement of, ***PS:*** 24
of Latimer, ***B:*** 128, 132
of McCoy, ***B:*** 154, 159
of Murray, ***B:*** 177
process for receiving, ***PS:*** 23
provision for, in Constitution, ***PS:*** 24–25
renewal of, ***PS:*** 24
for sewing machine, *A:* 52
Patroon system
B: 12
Pawtucket, Rhode Island, Brown's Mill in
A: 2 (ill.), 11, 12, 45
Peabody, George, & Company
B: 164
Pennsylvania Gazette (newspaper)
PS: 137
Pennsylvania Railroad
A: 79, 91, 139
B: 32–33, 36
PS: 138
Pennsylvania Society for the Encouragement of Manufactures and the Useful Arts
PS: 13
Pension system, creation of first funded, for workers
B: 36–37
People's Party of America
A: 179–80
B: 139
Perkins, Frances
B: 107
labor movement and, ***PS:*** 169
Perkins, Joan
A: 50
Perseverance (steamboat)
B: 77
Philadelphia and Reading Coal and Iron Company
A: 139
Philadelphia, Pennsylvania
A: 102
population in, *A:* 7
railroads serving, *A:* 22
streetcars in, *A:* 107
textile production in, *A:* 11
Philanthropy
A: 94
of Carnegie, *A:* 94
of Morgan, *A:* 94
of Rockefeller, *A:* 94
of Swift, *A:* 94
Phonautograph
B: 24
Phonograph
B: 66–67
Photography, developments in
PS: 106
Pierce Arrow
B: 95
Pilgrim's Progress (Bunyan)
B: 229
Pinchot, Gifford
A: 190
Pinkerton Detective Agency
A: 80, 93, 139, 147
B: 35

Pittsburgh, Pennsylvania
growth of, ***A:*** 103
immigrant populations in, ***PS:*** 101
labor violence in, ***A:*** 139
settlement of, ***A:*** 19
Plains Indians
A: 170
Plato
B: 122
Plessy v. Ferguson
B: 183, 250
Political cartoons
A: 74 (ill.)
PS: 137
Carnegie, Andrew as subject of, ***PS:*** 137–38, 142, 143 (ill.)
of Franklin, Benjamin, ***PS:*** 137
of Nast, Thomas, ***PS:*** 137, 145
Rockefeller, John D. as subject of, ***PS:*** 110, 137–38, 142, 144 (ill.)
trusts as targets of, ***PS:*** 137–38
Poll tax
B: 250
Pools
A: 87–88
PS: 151
Poor, gap between rich and
A: 108–10
Population growth
A: 100–1
Populist movement
B: 112
end of, ***B:*** 142–43
role of Lease in, ***B:*** 140–42
Populist Party
A: 165, 179
B: 112–13
formation of, ***B:*** 139
platform of, ***A:*** 179–80
Port Huron
B: 62
Postal service, advances in
A: 23–24
Postindustrial era
A: 215–16
Poverty line, defining
B: 105
Powderly, Terence
A: 140, 140 (ill.)
Power loom
A: 45–46, 47
B: 146, 147
PS: 30
Pre–Civil War economy
A: 153–55, 153 (ill.)
Primary system
B: 113
Problem of Civilization Solved, The (Lease)
B: 143
Process chart
B: 98
Progressive, The (magazine)
B: 112
Progressive Era
A: 182–96
B: 7, 19
PS: 129
drive to regulate big business, ***A:*** 184–85
muckrakers in, ***A:*** 185–87
reforms at state level, ***A:*** 193–96
Wilson's reforms of, ***A:*** 192–93
Progressive movement
B: 229
achievements of, ***B:*** 113
Progressive Party
A: 192
B: 7
in election of 1924, ***B:*** 117–18, 118 (ill.)
founding of, ***B:*** 109, 112–13
Jane Addams as delegate to national convention, ***B:*** 7
Progressive tax
B: 114
Prohibition
B: 143
Promontory Point (Utah)
A: 74
PS: 74
Psychology of Industrial Management, The (Gilbreth)
B: 93
Public education
A: 124
Public land, granting to railroads
A: 71–72
Public School Art Society
B: 221
Puck (magazine)
PS: 137
Pujo Money Trust Investigation Committee
B: 172
Pulleys
A: 33
Pullman car
A: 81, 81 (ill.)
B: 53
Pullman Company
B: 53, 55, 186, 187
Pullman, George
A: 81, 81 (ill.), 144
B: 33, 52–53, 186
Pullman, Illinois
A: 144
B: 52–53
Pullman Strike
A: 144–46
collapse of, ***A:*** 146; ***B:*** 56
media coverage of, ***B:*** 55–56
Pure Food and Drug Act (1906)
A: 187

Q

Quadricycle
B: 82–83
Quakers
B: 101, 148

R

R. J. Reynolds
A: 159
Race Ideals (Murray)
B: 180
Racial discrimination, Debs's interest in ending
B: 52
Ragged Dick
PS: **181–93,** 182 (ill.)
excerpt from *Ragged Dick, or, Street Life in New York with the Boot-Blacks* (Alger), ***PS:*** 187–90
Rags-to-riches story
A: 84
Rags-to-riches theme
PS: 181, 192, 205
Railroad Brotherhoods
A: 144, 146

Railroad industry, need for regulation
PS: 150
Railroad spikes
A: 72–73
Railroads
A: 15
1877 strike in, *A:* 79–80, 80 (ill.)
advances in, *A:* 20–23, 21 (ill.)
building of, *PS:* 69
Chinese immigrants work on, *PS:* 71, 73–74
competition in, *A:* 80, 82
construction of transcontinental, *PS:* 73–74, 77
costs of farming and, *A:* 177–78
growth of, *A:* 60–61
impact on farming in Old Northwest, *A:* 167–69
increase in construction, *A:* 68, 70
innovations in, *A:* 78
Interstate Commerce and, *A:* 97–98
management of, *A:* 77–79
modernization of operations, *A:* 78–79
refrigeration technology in, *A:* 88
role of J. P. Morgan in, *B:* 165–66
scientific management and, *B:* 93–94
steam locomotive in, *A:* 24
Vanderbilt and, *B:* 239–41
water closets on, *B:* 130
in Western Settlement, *A:* 169–70
Randolph, A. Philip
A: 150
***B:* 182–92**, 183 (ill.)
Congress for Industrial Organization (CIO) and, *B:* 189
early ambitions of, *B:* 183–85
education of, *B:* 184
March on Washington Movement for Jobs and Freedom and, *B:* 182, 190–92
marriage of, *B:* 184
as Socialist, *B:* 184–85
union activities of, *B:* 186–87, 192
writings and public speaking by, *B:* 185
Randolph, James
B: 183
Randolph, Lucille Green
B: 184–85
Random Reminiscences
***PS:* 109–23**
excerpt from *Random Reminiscences of Men and Events* (Rockefeller), *PS:* 119–21
memoir as defense of Rockefeller, *PS:* 110
Real McCoy, meaning of term
B: 158–59
Reaper
A: 37–38
Reconstruction Act (1867)
B: 177–78
Reconstruction Era, South in
A: 155–56
Regulatory laws, Progressive support for
B: 113
Religious Society of Friends
B: 101, 148
Remington Typewriter Company
B: 95
Remington-Rand
A: 213, 214
Report and Findings of the Joint Committee to Investigate the "Sweat Shop" System (Kelley)
B: 105
Report to Congress on the Subject of Manufacturers. See Congressional Report on Manufactures
Republican legislation, during Civil War
A: 59–62
Republican Party, policy toward businesses
A: 62
Republicanism, Jefferson's support for
PS: 1
Rest break
B: 94
Retirement plans, nonexistence of
A: 117
Revolution, The (newspaper)
PS: 48
Revolvers
A: 39
Rich, gap between poor and
A: 108–10
Richards, Fannie
B: 160
Richmond, Virginia, damage to, in American Civil War
A: 155
Riis, Jacob
A: 111–12
B: 228
PS: 97–107, 99 (ill.)
death of, *PS:* 106
drawings and photographs of, *PS:* 98 (ill.), 99–100, 100 (ill.), 106, 107
early life of, *PS:* 97
excerpt from *How the Other Half Lives* by, *PS:* 102–3
friendship with T. Roosevelt, *PS:* 105
immigration to New York City, *PS:* 97–98
investigations into living conditions, *PS:* 100
as newspaper reporter, *PS:* 98–100
Rillieux, Norbert
B: 178–79
The Rise of Silas Lapham
***PS:* 194–205**
excerpts from *The Rise of Silas Lapham* (Howells), *PS:* 199–203
River traffic
A: 17
Roads, early U.S.
A: 14, 15 (ill.), 16–17
Robber barons
A: 84–99, 182
PS: 66, 88, 137, 148
J. P. Morgan as, *B:* 162
Robinson, Harriet Hanson
PS: 30–38, 31 (ill.), 32 (ill.)
appearance before Select Committee on Woman Suffrage, *PS:* 36–37
early life, *PS:* 32
excerpt from *Loom and Spindle: or, Life among the Early Mill Girls* by, *PS:* 34–36

experience as mill worker, ***PS:*** 32–33
marriage of, ***PS:*** 36
memoirs of, ***PS:*** 33
Robinson, William Stevens
PS: 36–37
Rochester, New York
PS: 53
Rockefeller, Alice
B: 197
Rockefeller, Alta
B: 197
Rockefeller, Bessie
B: 197
Rockefeller Center
B: 200
Rockefeller, Edith
B: 197
Rockefeller, Eliza Davison
B: 194–95
Rockefeller Foundation
A: 94
B: 200, 205–6
PS: 122, 146
Rockefeller Institute for Medical Research
A: 94
B: 200, 205
PS: 122, 146
Rockefeller, John D.
A: 64, 158, 185–86
B: **193–206,** 194 (ill.), 204 (ill.)
PS: 109–23, 111 (ill.), 148, 181, 198
as Baptist, ***B:*** 197–98
breakup of Standard Oil Company of New Jersey of, ***PS:*** 94
childhood of, ***B:*** 194–95
creation of Standard Oil Trust, ***A:*** 88–91; ***B:*** 193, 201
death of, ***B:*** 206
early life of, ***PS:*** 111, 139–40
education of, ***B:*** 195
employment of, ***B:*** 196
excerpt from *Random Reminiscences of Men and Events* by, ***PS:*** 119–21
expanding into oil refining, ***A:*** 89
expansion into international market, ***PS:*** 114
family of, ***B:*** 197–98
founding of Standard Oil, ***PS:*** 109
in oil industry, ***B:*** 196–97, 201–3
participation in South Improvement Company scheme, ***PS:*** 112–13
personal fortune, ***PS:*** 122
philanthropy of, ***A:*** 94; ***B:*** 193, 204–6; ***PS:*** 122, 134, 146
philosophy of, ***PS:*** 112, 116–17
political cartoons of, ***PS:*** 110, 137–38, 142, 144
provision of financial assistance to J. P. Morgan, ***B:*** 171
public attacks on, ***PS:*** 122–23
purchase of stock in other companies, ***PS:*** 114–15
retirement from Standard Oil Company, ***PS:*** 116, 122, 146
Sherman Antitrust Act and, ***B:*** 227
Standard Oil monopoly and, ***B:*** 198–200, 223, 228–29
Tidewater Pipe Line Company and, ***PS:*** 113–14
wealth of, ***PS:*** 88
Rockefeller, John Davidson, Jr.
B: 197, 200
Rockefeller, Laura Celestia Spelman
B: 197
Rockefeller Sanitary Commission for Eradication of Hookworm Disease
B: 205
Rockefeller, William
PS: 114–15
Rockefeller, William Avery
B: 194–95, 199, 201
Roland, Madame
B: 226
Roosevelt, Eleanor
B: 188–90
Roosevelt, Franklin Delano
A: 208 (ill.)
appointment of Perkins as labor secretary, ***B:*** 107
cabinet of, ***B:*** 220
civil rights and, ***B:*** 182
executive order signed by, ***B:*** 189
Great Depression and, ***B:*** 119
labor movement and, ***PS:*** 169
labor relations and, ***B:*** 187
New Deal and, ***A:*** 207–9; ***B:*** 107
New Deal legislation under, ***PS:*** 178–79
Roosevelt, Theodore
A: 187 (ill.)
B: 37, 252
PS: 69
antitrust actions of, ***A:*** 187–89
antitrust movement and, ***B:*** 115–16, 171; ***PS:*** 157, 158
coining of muckraker term, ***A:*** 185; ***B:*** 229
Conservation movement and, ***A:*** 190
creation of Department of Commerce and Labor, ***A:*** 191
investigation of Standard Oil monopoly, ***PS:*** 129
labor unions and, ***A:*** 150
reforms of, ***A:*** 187–89, 191
Riis and, ***PS:*** 105
visit to Hull House, ***B:*** 7
Root, Elisha K.
A: 35
Rosenwald, Julius
B: 252
Rouge Ford plant
B: 86–88, 87 (ill.)
Roving
A: 47
Ruffner, Lewis
B: 246, 247
Rugoff, Milton
B: 10
Rule of reason
A: 189
Rumsey, James
A: 18, 33
B: 76, 77
PS: 27
Rustin, Bayard
B: 191

S

San Francisco, California
Chinese immigrants in ***B:*** 43–44
immigrants in, ***A:*** 105
streetcars in, ***A:*** 107

San Francisco, Chinese workers in,
PS: 74, 75
San Francisco Riot (1876)
PS: 77
Sanders, Thomas
B: 24, 26
Santa Fe Railroad
A: 171
Satire
PS: 146
SBC
B: 28
Schlesinger, Arthur, Jr.
A: 205
Schneiderman, Rose
A: 129
Science (magazine)
B: 28
Scientific management
A: 200–1
B: 89, 92–93, 231
Scott, Leon
B: 24
Scott, Thomas
B: 32
Scott, Thomas A.
PS: 138
Scranton, Pennsylvania, immigrants in
A: 105
Seaman's Act (1915)
B: 116
Sears, Roebuck
B: 252
"A Second Peep at Factory Life" (Baker)
excerpt from, *PS:* 43–46
Select Committee on Woman Suffrage
PS: 36–37
Senate Armed Services Committee
B: 190
Seneca Chief (packet boat)
PS: 51
Separate but equal philosophy
B: 250
Servicemen's Readjustment Act (1944)
A: 210–11
Settlement houses. *See also* Hull House; Toynbee Hall
B: 8
Sewers
A: 114
Sewing machine
A: 52 (ill.)
adaptation of, to shoemaking, *A:* 54
invention of, *A:* 51, 52
Shame of the Cities (Steffens)
B: 228
Sharecroppers
B: 250
Sharecropping
A: 159–60
Shelby Steel Tube Company
B: 169
Sheppard-Towner Act (1921)
B: 106–7, 125
Sherman Antitrust Act (1890)
A: 98–99, 148, 184, 188–89
B: 170, 171, 202, 203, 227–28
PS: 94, 116, 121, 144, 145, 149, 153–54
amendments to, *PS:* 158–59
enforcement of, *PS:* 157–58
excerpt from, *PS:* 156–57
vague wording of, *PS:* 154
Sherman, John
A: 98
PS: 153, 153 (ill.)
Sherman Silver Purchase Act
B: 111
Shipping industry, role of Francis Cabot Lowell in
B: 144–46
Shoe industry
A: 52–55, 54 (ill.)
Shuttle
A: 4, 47
Siemens, Charles William
A: 92
Siemens-Martin open-hearth method
A: 78, 92
Sierra Nevada Mountains
A: 73, 106
Simpson College
B: 248
Sinclair, Upton
A: 186–87
B: 107, 228
Singer, Isaac M.
A: 52
Sioux Indians
A: 170
Sixteenth Amendment
A: 85
Sixty-hour week
A: 193
Skibo Castle
B: 38 (ill.)
Skilled craftsmen
A: 119–20
Slater, Esther Parkinson
B: 214
Slater, Hannah Wilkinson
B: 212
Slater, John
B: 212
Slater mill
A: 2 (ill.)
B: 212–14, 213 (ill.)
Slater, Samuel
A: 45
B: **207–14**, 208 (ill.)
PS: 14, 15
at Arkwright Mills, *B:* 149
death of, *B:* 214
mill of, *B:* 212–14, 213 (ill.)
textile industry and, *A:* 11–12; *B:* 207–11
Slater, Samuel, & Company
B: 212–14
Slater, William
B: 207–8
Slavery as issue in Civil War
A: 1–2, 39
B: 156, 196
Sliver
A: 47
Slums
A: 104
Smallpox
A: 127
B: 104
Smith, Adam
A: 62–63, 62 (ill.)
PS: 117
Smith, Page
A: 68
Social changes, in England
A: 6–7
Social Darwinism
A: 95–96, 111
PS: 86, 95
Social Democratic Party, creation of
B: 57

A = Development of the Industrial U.S.: Almanac—
B = Development of the Industrial U.S.: Biographies

Social reform photography
PS: 107
Social Security Act
A: 208
Socialism
B: 107, 221
Debs and, *B:* 56–57
Socialist Party of America (SPA)
A: 143
B: 59, 184–85, 188, 221
Debs as member of, *A:* 146
Society As I Have Found It (McAllister)
B: 14 (ill.)
Society for the Prevention of Cruelty to Animals
PS: 192
Sojourners
B: 41–43
Sole proprietorship
B: 147
South
A: 152
African Americans migration North, *A:* 163
new industries in, *A:* 157
plantation system of, *A:* 153 (ill.), 155
pre–Civil War economy, *A:* 153–55, 153 (ill.)
Reconstruction in, *A:* 155–56
sharecropping in, *A:* 159–60
Southern Alliance in, *A:* 164–65
tenant farming, *A:* 159–60
tobacco industry in, *A:* 157–59
Tuskegee Institute in, *A:* 161–64
South Improvement Company
A: 89–91
B: 225–26
PS: 112–13, 126–27, 130, 135
Southern Alliance
A: 164–65, 178, 179
Southern Christian Leadership Conference (SCLC)
B: 191
Southern Power System
A: 159
Southwestern Bell of Texas
B: 28
Spencer, Herbert
A: 95, 95 (ill.)
PS: 86, 86 (ill.)
Spencer-Churchill, Charles
B: 242
Spencer-Churchill, Consuelo Vanderbilt
B: 242
Sperry Rand
A: 213
Spinners
A: 3–4
Spinning frame
A: 4, 12
Spinning jenny
A: 4, 5 (ill.)
B: 209
Spinning machine
A: 4, 118 (ill.)
Spinning, mechanization of
A: 4
Spinning wheel
A: 12
Spinster
PS: 37
St. James Methodist Episcopal Church (Chicago)
A: 94
St. Lawrence River
PS: 59
St. Lawrence Seaway
PS: 58–59
St. Louis, Missouri
growth of, *A:* 167–68
settlement of, *A:* 19
Standard Oil Company
A: 88–89, 98, 186, 189
B: 199, 223
capacity of, *PS:* 114
charter of, as corporation in state of Ohio, *PS:* 111
competition and, *PS:* 111–12
development of pipeline system, *A:* 90–91
expansion into international market, *PS:* 114
founding of, *PS:* 109
as monopoly, *B:* 198–200
operating practices of, *PS:* 110
purchase of stock in other companies, *PS:* 114–15
reputation of, *PS:* 109–10
retirement of Rockefeller from, *PS:* 116
South Improvement Company and, *A:* 89–91; *PS:* 126–27
Tarbell's exposé of, *B:* 227–30
violation of Sherman Act by, *PS:* 116, 121–22
Standard Oil Company of California
B: 203
PS: 122
Standard Oil Company of Indiana
B: 203
PS: 122
Standard Oil Company of New Jersey
B: 201, 203
PS: 115, 122
breakup of, *PS:* 94
Standard Oil Company of New York
B: 203
PS: 122
Standard Oil Company of Ohio
B: 203
PS: 122
Standard Oil refinery
PS: 110 (ill.)
Standard Oil Trust
A: 88–91, 158
B: 193, 201
PS: 124
creation of, *A:* 91; *PS:* 115, 141, 152
dissolution of, *B:* 230
focus of Tarbell's articles on, *PS:* 133–34
growth of, *PS:* 139–42
power of, *PS:* 115–16
as target of political cartoons, *PS:* 137–38
Standard Oil v. United States
PS: 145
Stanford, Leland
A: 71, 74
B: 40
Stanton, Elizabeth Cady
PS: 47–48
Starr, Caleb
B: 216
Starr, Eliza Allen
B: 216
Starr, Ellen Gates
***B:* 215–22**
Addams and, *B:* 216–18, 220
art interests of, *B:* 216, 218–19, 221
as eccentric, *B:* 221

family influence, ***B:*** 215–16
at Hull House with Jane Addams, ***B:*** 4, 6, 121
illness and death of, ***B:*** 221
in labor movement, ***B:*** 219–21
Starr, Susan Gates Childs
B: 216
State level, reforms at
A: 193–96
Steam engines
A: 18
B: 82
early, ***A:*** 5–6, 6 (ill.)
Steam-engine locomotive
A: 24
B: 78
Steamboats
A: 15, 18–19, 19 (ill.)
advances in, ***B:*** 74–77, 75 (ill.)
patents on, ***PS:*** 27–28
Steel
A: 91
in England, ***A:*** 4–5
innovations in technology, ***A:*** 147–48
U.S. production of, prior to 1865, ***A:*** 39
Steel cartel
B: 36
Steel industry
B: 33–35
growth of, ***PS:*** 138–39
Steel plow
A: 38–39
Steffens, Lincoln
A: 185, 186, 186 (ill.)
B: 55
as muckraker, ***B:*** 228
Stephens, Uriah S.
A: 136–37
Stephenson, George
A: 20
Stereo-cyclegraph
B: 94
Stevens, Alzina
B: 125
Stevens, John
A: 18, 20, 24
Stevens, Robert Livingston
A: 23, 24
Stock market
1929 crash of, ***A:*** 206
Black Friday and, ***A:*** 66
Stockton & Darlington Railway
A: 20
Story of My Life and Work, The (Washington)
B: 244
Story of the Negro (Washington)
B: 159
Street Arabs
PS: 183, 184 (ill.)
Streetcars
A: 107
Strikes
defined, ***A:*** 137, 189
Great, of 1877, ***A:*** 139–40
Homestead, ***A:*** 92–93, 146–48
McCormick, ***A:*** 141–42
Pullman, ***A:*** 137
railroad, ***A:*** 79–80, 80 (ill.)
during World War I, ***A:*** 148, 150
Study of Sociology, The (Spencer)
PS: 86
Strobridge, James
B: 44
Strouse, Jean
B: 162
Strutt, Jebediah
A: 11
B: 208–9
Student and Schoolmate (magazine)
PS: 184
Suburbs
A: 104–5
Sullivan, Louis
A: 115
Summer School of Scientific Management
B: 95
Sumner, William Graham
A: 96
PS: 84–95, 88 (ill.), 107
belief in concentration of wealth, ***PS:*** 94
education of, ***PS:*** 85
excerpt from *The Concentration of Wealth* by, ***PS:*** 90–93
philosophy of, ***PS:*** 84, 85 (ill.), 93, 94–95, 95
positive view of society, ***PS:*** 87
writings of, ***PS:*** 86–87, 93
at Yale, ***PS:*** 85–86, 87
Supreme Court, U.S., rule of reason and
A: 189
Survival of the fittest
A: 95–96
Swan, Joseph Wilson
B: 67
Sweatshops
A: 127–29
PS: 170
in New York City, ***PS:*** 163–64
Swift, Gustavus
A: 88
philanthropy of, ***A:*** 94
Sylvis, William
A: 136
Symonds, Eliza Grace
B: 22–23

T

Taft, William Howard
appointment of Lathrop as director of Children's Bureau, ***B:*** 125
creation of Children's Bureau by, ***B:*** 106
defeat by Woodrow Wilson, ***B:*** 116
Washington, Booker T., and, ***B:*** 252
Taft, William Howard, antitrust movement under, ***PS:*** 158
in election of 1912, ***A:*** 191–92
Taiping Rebellion (1851–64)
B: 41
Tammany Hall
A: 110
B: 239
Taoism
B: 42
Tarbell, Elizabeth McCullough
B: 223–24
Tarbell, Frank
PS: 126
Tarbell, Franklin Sumner
B: 223–26
Tarbell, Ida M.
A: 185–86
B: **223–32**, 224 (ill.)
PS: 116, 124–35, 125 (ill.)
articles of, in *McClure's*, ***PS:*** 127–28
autobiography of, ***B:*** 232
childhood of, ***B:*** 223–24
death of, ***B:*** 232

early life of, ***PS:*** 124, 126
education of, ***B:*** 226–27; ***PS:*** 126–27
excerpt from *The History of Standard Oil* by, ***PS:*** 130–33
exposé of Standard Oil by, ***B:*** 227–30
introduction to oil business, ***B:*** 223–26
investigative series at *McClure's* by, ***B:*** 202–3
labor movement and, ***B:*** 231–32
life after *McClure's,* ***B:*** 230–31
at *McClure's,* ***B:*** 226–30
as muckraker, ***B:*** 55
on rights and roles of women, ***B:*** 232
Tariff in Our Times, The (Tarbell)
B: 230
Tariff Act (1890)
B: 111
Tariffs
A: 10, 60
B: 151
Tarbell on, ***B:*** 230–31
Taylor, Frederick Winslow
A: 200, 200 (ill.)
B: 92–93, 231
Taylorism
A: 200–1, 202
B: 92–94, 231
Teachers Insurance and Annuity Association-College Retirement Equities Fund (TIAA-CREF)
B: 38
Teapot Dome scandal
B: 117
Telegrams
A: 26 (ill.)
Telegraph operator
B: 62–63
Telegraph system
PS: 89–90
Telegraphs, in communication
A: 24–26, 26 (ill.)
Telephone
B: 21
invention of, ***B:*** 21, 27–28
milestones in history of, ***B:*** 26
transmitter and receiver of Bell's first, ***B:*** 25 (ill.)
Temple, Lewis
B: 179
Ten Hours Movement
PS: 47
Ten-footers
A: 53
Ten-hour workday
A: 123, 193
PS: 172
Tenant farming
A: 159–60
Tenement buildings
A: 108–9, 109 (ill.)
Terry, Eli, mass-produced clocks of
A: 34
Tesla, Nikola
B: 69
Tetrahedral kite
B: 28
Textile industry
English, ***A:*** 3–4, 10
establishment of, ***A:*** 45–47
in Lowell, Massachusetts, ***A:*** 43 (ill.)
Samuel Slater and, ***A:*** 11–12
women workers in, ***B:*** 150–51
working conditions in, ***B:*** 148–49, 151
Textile mills, child workers in
PS: 15
Textile technology, Lowell's study of
B: 146–47
Therblig
B: 95
Theory of the Leisure Class, The (Veblen)
B: 16–17
Thomas, Abel C.
PS: 41
Thomson, J. Edgar, Works
B: 33
Thoreau, Henry David, founding of *Atlantic Monthly* by
PS: 195
Tidewater Pipe Line Company
PS: 113–14
Titan: The Life of John D. Rockefeller, Sr. (Chernow)
B: 197
PS: 113, 117
Titanic (ship)
B: 116
Titusville, Pennsylvania, discovery of oil in
B: 224–25
Tobacco industry, James Buchanan Duke and
A: 157–59
Toynbee Hall
A: 112
B: 3, 217
Transcontinental railroad
A: 69 (ill.), 70–72
B: 44–45
PS: 77
building first, ***A:*** 60, 72–74
completion of, ***A:*** 69 (ill.)
construction of, ***PS:*** 73–74
Transportation
canals in, ***A:*** 19–20
early roads in, ***A:*** 15 (ill.), 16–17
importance of, ***A:*** 14–16
limitations in early, ***A:*** 7
railroads in, ***A:*** 20–23, 21 (ill.)
river traffic in, ***A:*** 17
steamboats in, ***A:*** 18–19, 19 (ill.)
Triangle Shirtwaist Company factory fire (1911)
A: 121, 127–29, 128 (ill.)
Triangle Shirtwaist Factory
PS: 161
fire at, ***PS:*** 167–68, 169 (ill.)
strikes at, ***PS:*** 165
workers at, as member of ILGWU, ***PS:*** 164–65
Trinity College
A: 159
Truman, Harry S.
B: 190
Trustees
PS: 136
Trusts
A: 87–88, 98, 182
B: 170–71
PS: 88, 118, 136
creation of, ***PS:*** 151–52
defined, ***B:*** 115
public dissatisfaction with power of, ***PS:*** 137
Standard Oil, ***A:*** 88–91, 158; ***B:*** 193, 201, 230; ***PS:*** 115–16, 124, 134–35, 138–42, 141, 152
steel, ***B:*** 174

as targets of political cartoons, *PS:* 137–38
Theodore Roosevelt's opposition to, *B:* 115–16
"A Trust Giant's Point of View" (ill.)
PS: 144
"A Trustworthy Beast" (ill.)
PS: 143
Tuberculosis
A: 122
Turnpikes
A: 16
Tuskegee Airmen
B: 252
Tuskegee Institute
A: 162 (ill.)
B: 244, 249 (ill.), 252
Carver at, *B:* 248;
Washington, Booker T. and, *A:* 161–64
Tuskegee Normal and Industrial Institute
B: 247
Tuskegee University
A: 161
Tuttleton, James W.
PS: 196–97
Twain, Mark
A: 57
B: 37
PS: 196, 204, 204 (ill.)
Tweed, William Marcy "Boss,"
A: 110–11, 111 (ill.)
PS: 145, 183
Twenty Years at Hull House (Addams)
B: 9
Two-party system
PS: 7
Typhoid
A: 127

U

Una (newspaper)
PS: 47
Underground Railroad
B: 154
Unemployment Conference
B: 231
Uniform gauges
A: 78
Union Labor Party, formation of
B: 138–39
Union Pacific Railroad
A: 71, 74, 187
B: 44, 47, 170
PS: 73
construction of, *A:* 72–73
Unitarianism
PS: 183
United Automobile Workers
B: 88
United Company of Philadelphia for Promoting American Manufactures
PS: 13
United Mine Workers (UMW)
A: 144, 149, 150, 191
United States
English restrictions on textile industry in, *A:* 10
industrialization of new, *A:* 7–8
visions of future, *A:* 8–10
United States Electric Lighting
B: 131, 132
United States Rubber
B: 95
United States Steel Corporation
B: 36, 169, 170, 174, 232
PS: 88, 145, 152
UNIVAC I
A: 213
Universal Automatic Computer
A: 213
Universal Negro Improvement Association
B: 185
Universal stock ticker
B: 64 (ill.), 65
Unskilled labor
A: 120
Up from Slavery (Washington)
B: 244
Uprising of 20,000
PS: 165
Urbanization. *See also* Cities
A: 100–115
farm migration and, *A:* 106–8
gap between rich and poor and, *A:* 108–10
immigration and, *A:* 105–6
trend toward, *A:* 100–103
U.S. Steel, J. P. Morgan and
A: 95
U.S.S. *Massasoit*
B: 130

V

Vail, Theodore N.
PS: 90
Vanderbilt, Alva
B: 17
Vanderbilt, Cornelius
A: 64, 74 (ill.), 94, 108
***B:* 234–43**, 235 (ill.)
PS: 65, 66–67, 69, 148, 181, 198
as corporate raider, *B:* 241–43
death of, *B:* 234, 241, 242
dislike of, by Carolyn Astor, *B:* 16–17
early life of, *B:* 234–36
Erie Canal and, *A:* 76
family of, *B:* 241–42
legal battles of, *B:* 237–38
profits from California gold rush, *B:* 238–39
railroad industry and, *B:* 239–41
in shipping business, *B:* 234–37
value of estate, *B:* 234
Vanderbilt, Cornelius, II
B: 242
Vanderbilt, Cornelius Jeremiah
B: 242
Vanderbilt, Frances Crawford
B: 241
Vanderbilt, Gloria
B: 242
Vanderbilt, Reginald Claypoole
B: 242
Vanderbilt, Sophia Johnson
B: 238, 241
Vanderbilt University
A: 94
B: 241
Vanderbilt, William
B: 166
Vanderbilt, William Henry
B: 241, 242
PS: 129
Vanderbilt, William K., II
B: 242
Veblen, Thorstein
B: 16, 17 (ill.)

Verdict, The (magazine)
PS: 137
Vertical expansion
A: 87
PS: 118
Virginia City, Nevada
A: 178
Visible speech
B: 22
Visible Speech: The Science of Universal Alphabets (Bell)
B: 23
Voice of Industry, The
PS: 41–42, 47
Voight, Henry
B: 75
Volta Laboratory
B: 27
Voting Rights Act (1965)
B: 179, 191

W

Wabash, St. Louis and Pacific Railway Company v. Illinois
PS: 153
Waiter Protective Association
B: 189
Wald, Lillian D.
B: 106
Waldorf-Astoria Hotel
B: 18
Waltham System
B: 150
Waltham-Lowell System
A: 46
War of 1812 (1812–15)
B: 151, 236
Warner, Charles Dudley
A: 57
Warp yarn
A: 47
Washington, Booker T.
B: 244–52, 245 (ill.)
Atlanta Compromise and, **B:** 250–51
autobiographies of, **B:** 244
death of, **B:** 252
dining by, at White House, **B:** 252
education of, **B:** 246–48
Latimer's correspondence with, **B:** 134
McCoy's mention in *Story of the Negro* by, **B:** 159
philosophy of self-sufficiency, **B:** 248–50
Tuskegee Institute and, **A:** 161–64; **B:** 244, 247–48
work in the mines, **B:** 245–46
Washington, D.C., Coxey's Army march on
B: 54–55
Washington, Fanny Norton
B: 247
Washington, George
B: 76
PS: 10–11
administration of, **PS:** 7
cabinet of, **PS:** 6–7
Hamilton as member of military staff of, **PS:** 11
Jefferson as secretary of state under, **A:** 9, 33
Washington, Margaret Murray
B: 160, 247–48
Washington, Olivia Davidson
B: 247
Washington, Portia
B: 247
Water Frame
B: 210
Watered-down stock
A: 74
Waterwheel
A: 4, 12, 47
B: 151
Watson, Thomas
B: 21, 24–26
Watt, James
A: 5–6, 6 (ill.), 18
B: 74
Wayland Seminary
B: 247
Ways of Women, The (Tarbell)
B: 232
Wealth Against Commonwealth (Lloyd)
A: 97
B: 104, 201, 228
PS: 94, 127
Weaver, James B.
A: 180
B: 142
Webb, Beatrice, visits by, to Hull House
B: 7–8
Webb, Sidney, visits by, to Hull House
B: 7–8
Weekly Herald, Edison's publication of
B: 62
Wells-Barnett, Ida
B: 250
Western Electric Company
B: 24
Western settlement
early turnpikes in, **A:** 16
railroads in, **A:** 169–70
Western Union Telegraph Company
B: 27, 63–64
Westinghouse Engine Company
B: 81, 134
Wheatley, Phillis, Home for Aged Colored Ladies
B: 159, 160
Wheatstone, Charles
A: 25
Wheeler, Burton K.
B: 117
Wheeler, Etta Angel
PS: 192
Whiskey ring scandal
PS: 63
Whitman, Walt
PS: 195
Whitney, Eli
A: 31–32, 34
PS: 14, 21–28, 24 (ill.)
cotton gin of, **A:** 36, 37 (ill.)
early life of, **PS:** 21–22
education of, **PS:** 21
invention of cotton gin, **PS:** 21, 23
manufacture of guns, **PS:** 26–27
partnership with Miller, **PS:** 24
text of Cotton Gin Petition by, **PS:** 21–28
Whitney, Gertrude Vanderbilt
B: 242
Whitney Museum of American Art
B: 242
Whitneyville
A: 31–32
Wilson, Woodrow
A: 192 (ill.)
in election of 1912, **A:** 192; **B:** 116

reforms of, ***A:*** 192–93
Tarbell and, ***B:*** 230–31
Wind power
B: 74
Wischnewetzky, Lazare
B: 102
Wisconsin Idea
B: 114–15
Wobblies
A: 148
Woman's Era, The (newspaper)
PS: 48
Women
in factories, ***A:*** 48, 49, 50, 118 (ill.), 125–26
in labor unions, ***A:*** 50
post World War II, ***A:*** 211–12
in World War II, ***A:*** 209–10
Women workers
in garment industry, ***PS:*** 162–64, 162 (ill.)
housing for, ***PS:*** 31–32, 37
labor unions exclusion of, ***PS:*** 163
Women's Bureau
A: 125–26
Women's International Peace League for Peace and Freedom
B: 9
Women's Peace Party
B: 9
Women's suffrage
B: 126, 160
PS: 134
Debs support for, ***B:*** 51
Women's Trade Union League (WTUL)
A: 125–26
B: 220
Woodruff Sleeping Car Company
B: 33
Work day, length of
A: 48
Work ethic
A: 45
Work stoppages. *See also* Strikes
A: 54–55
Workers, abuse of, by industrialists
PS: 1, 2 (ill.)
Workers' associations, opposition to child labor
A: 123
Workers' compensation
A: 136, 196
Workers' compensation laws
B: 114
Workforce
children in, ***A:*** 11, 45, 121–25, 122(ill.), 194–95, 194 (ill.); ***B:*** 100, 104, 116, 126, 213–14
diversity of, ***A:*** 135–36
growth of industrial, ***B:*** 49
hierarchy in, ***A:*** 119–20
immigrants in, ***A:*** 126–27
in industrial age, ***A:*** 117–31
women in, ***A:*** 48, 49, 50, 118 (ill.), 125–26
working conditions of, ***B:*** 49
Working hours
A: 123, 193–94
PS: 172–80
Workingman's Party
PS: 77, 80–81
Workweek, length of
A: 120
World War I (1914–18)
Debs opposition to, ***B:*** 58
Ford and, ***B:*** 85–86
industry after, ***A:*** 205
La Follette's opposition to, ***B:*** 116–17
strikes during, ***A:*** 148, 150
World War II (1939–45)
A: 209–12
women in, ***A:*** 209–10
World War II, United States entrance into
PS: 81

Y

Yellow Peril
B: 47
PS: 76
Yost, Edna
B: 98
Young Men's Christian Association (YMCA)
A: 94
PS: 183
Young, Owen D.
B: 232